忠孝虎

勇往直前

陸正平 題

WE CAN DO

BY

MOSHE KAI CAVALIN

www.bookstandpublishing.com

Published by
Bookstand Publishing
Morgan Hill, CA
3475_3

ISBN 978-1-61863-045-2

Printed in the United States of America

CONTENTS

This book is dedicated to:

The ALMIGHTY WHO showered me with many Blessings,

My Parents and Grandparents who demonstrated a profound Love and

My Teachers that provided me with Unswerving Knowledge.

My sincere acknowledgement to my masters, teachers, mentors, friends and counselors:

Ms. Nabuko Fujimoto.	Dr. Richard Moyer.	Prof. Richard Avila.
Master Zhen Ping Lu.	Prof. & Sifu Dr. Chivey Wu.	Prof. Guojao Liao.
Prof. Daniel Judge.	Prof. Gabriel Castro.	Prof. Ken Teh.
Prof. Dr. Amir H. Sharifi.	Prof. Eagle Zhuang.	Prof. Adam Zheng.
Prof. Lucy Nargizian.	Prof. Cory Youngblood.	Prof. Viken Kiledjian.
Prof. Carlos B. Vasquez.	Prof. Dr. Linda Elias.	Prof. Fernando Jimenez.
Prof. Melissa Hendrata.	Prof. Juan Flores.	Prof. Liliana Urrutia.
ELAC Math Lab Crew.	Prof. Peter Petersen.	Prof. James Ralston.
Prof. Christian Haesemeyer.	Prof. Liancheng Chief.	Prof. Dr. Vanessa L. White.
Prof. K. G. White.	Mr. Mario Villegas.	Mr. Eddy Villanueva.
Mr. Mike Burgos.	Ms. Alejandra Ramirez.	Ms. Donna Cheng.
Ms. Ling-Mei Lein.	Ms. Cathy Behrens.	Ms. Bonnie Sherman.
Mr. Masaki Nakamura.	Mr. Jorge Chavez.	Mr. Thierry Hassid.
Mr. Kerry Sun.	Mr. Yemin Han.	Mr. Lin Kaung.
Mr. Hai Nguyen.	Mr. Alexander Carlos.	Mr. Rafael Alvarez.
Mr. Armando Rivera.	Mr. Israel Romero.	TA Adam Massey.
TA Zhang Hammo.	TA Benjamin Krause.	Sifu & TA Art Schonfeld.
Prof. & Sifu Jason Tsou.	Sifu Yudeng.	Sifu David Sha.
Sifu Nan Li.		

Special thanks: Ms. Elizabeth Musgrave and Ms. Nicole Grace.

Cover Calligraphy by Master Zhen Ping Lu.

Moshe Kai Cavalin

www.moshekai.com   kaihsiaohu@yahoo.com

 vii

FOREWORD

I reached a point that many people considered impossible for my age. The youngest Chinese student to enter the first year of a university in China was twelve years old. I was eight years old when I entered college. I completed my second year of university in the U.S. (A.A. Degree) when I was eleven years old. I finished with a flawless grade point average in all subjects taken. I was the top student in all my classes, above all of my older classmates. I entered as a junior at the University of California Los Angeles at the age of twelve years old. I will be finishing the Bachelor's Degree in Mathematics at UCLA probably at the age of 14 or 15 depending on my other projects. I reached as high as the moon, but anybody who really tries can reach beyond the Milky Way.

I wrote this book to help parents encourage their children to reach for the stars. If one pursues a dream, it is possible that anyone can get there and beyond. Many people think that I am a super genius or an alien being from a faraway galaxy. I am neither. Trust me; I am just a typically average kid. I love to collect toy cars and baseball caps. I love to eat pizza, sweets, play soccer, and read science books. Any kid or teenager can do as well as I did or even better. What separates me from the pack, however, is the cohesive and loving bond I share with my parents and a willingness to pursue our hopes and beliefs with a resilient heart.

Maybe someone does not have the same type of opportunities that I had, but if one gives an honest good try he/she will be successful on any level. The progress may be faster or slower than mine, but gradually the change becomes visible and the improvement will accelerate to a mach speed. **Perseverance and Resilience** are the keys. Many times I felt defeated and discouraged, thinking that I would never achieve the goals that I intended for myself. With determination and resolve, though, I bounced back. When one least expects it, the fruits of his/her efforts spring forth, and one will feel the satisfaction of success.

The first result took what seemed to me a long time, but when it happened, it was like a Fourth of July celebration inside of my head. Mental fireworks went off. After that, good tides seemed to arrive frequently. In the end, these merry accomplishments encouraged me to achieve a higher level of self-realization.

When we are born, we basically all start out from different levels in the playing field because we have different backgrounds, surroundings, and physical capabilities. The goal is to reach a higher platform of self-realization and enjoyment. Let me use an analogy to explain: We are maybe located in different life stations due to our personal circumstances. To travel to a better life, we can go by airplane, bus, or foot. It is up to us to choose the moment to depart, the route to take, and the manner in which to go. Allocating some time to plan the trip and what we want to accomplish is of the maximum importance. Parents, being more experienced on the facts of life, should participate with love and care in this very important endeavor. The parents serve as tour guides informing us, giving opinions, and comparing the choices and their future consequences.

For instance, if one goes by plane, maybe a wild storm will generate a rough ride; one may feel queasy, nervous, and stressed. That person will be confined inside of the airplane for the entire journey and the freedom is restricted. The pleasurable endeavors are curtailed by the activities on the airplane (that is, one is limited to the strategy defined and cannot give up much to distractions). One must realize that this impediment is for a short time, but it will produce a hefty progress. The early arrival will crown one's effort and it will give the untimely traveler chances to bask in the sun, collecting the richness of success before the others are even able to arrive. I decided to follow this path.

By bus, the trip will take a little longer, but we can have many stops to appease the boredom and we can have opportunities to dedicate time for pleasurable things that one may like. Less effort is needed on this trip. Ultimately, the arrival to destination will be in a later time. Using the bus, one still will be ahead of the game because the goal is to reach the destination in a secure and fast manner and arrive ahead of the mainstream.

The majority of parents in this world walks to their destination and lets their children do the same. Their future destination is vaguely planned or not at all. This is the norm. The parents step back and let the environment and the schools take over and educate their offspring. Without the parents' guidance, most of the kids, during their walk, get lost in the multitude, without destination and become a product of the surroundings, imitating the ones that they perceive as models around them. A few are lucky by choosing the right models, but most fail miserably. My heart is heavy when I

 x

see gang bangers and kids without direction throwing and trashing their lives away or ending up in jail. Their parents did not direct them to a constructive life due to many reasons. Their role models became strangers with misguided friendship, replacing the much sought parents' love and guidance. These kids become "losers" and our world loses much more.

I wrote this book hoping that parents step up their efforts and guide their children on their life journey. Perhaps, with this book, I may help some teens to look inside of their selves for strength to change their hearts and gather the willpower necessary to achieve "unachievable heights." Many people think that it is impossible to graduate at an early age or even graduate at all, let alone succeed in any aspiration and venture. It is not impossible. I did it, and I am not a superman or a genius. I am just a kid who executed a traced strategy heartily.

Don't waste time. Our sojourn in this life is brief. When we open our eyes, we may have already passed the prime time to succeed or the time to help our children. We become old and the children have already gone down the wrong path which has no return.

To Parents: Mark your presence in the life of the children by helping their progress and averting their suffering. With care, love, and resolve you are capable to propitiate a bright future to the children; in return, your offspring will find out the happiness from the deeds of an action well done and you will have the love of your children. Involve yourself with the future of your offspring, working together and helping them with love and perseverance.

To My Young Brothers and Sisters: If your parents are not cheering you on or giving you the support you need, the journey will be more challenging. Fighting alone will be tough but **I believe in you**. **Be strong**. The winner is the one who has the mind to think and the heart to believe and persevere. Fight on, jump over the hurdles and your future life will be much easier and rewarding. Be tough even though you are crying inside.

To All: Do not feel discouraged. I beg you please to consider the words of the great Muhammad Ali: "I hated every minute of training, but I said, 'Don't quit. Suffer now and live the rest of your life as a champion'".

INTRODUCTION

If there is any credit for writing this book, it belongs to my parents' and my masters' teachings. If there are any errors, I ask for forgiveness since between my ears dwells a very desolate tract. Seeing so many young students lost and perplexed with the educational maze and no route to follow, I felt an overwhelming pressure, responsibility and desire to help, to extend my hand to my young siblings. The best way that I can see helping is to write a book explaining how I went about to accomplish many things considered impossible. There are many ways to succeed and a resilient heart with a good plan will do the job.

I believe that each creature put in this planet is like a diamond in the rough. It is up to us to make it shine or not.

I am very thankful for the advice, corrections, revisions and help given to turn this book into a reality

CHAPTER 1:

BIRTH - VALENTINE'S DAY TIGER CUB

I was born on Valentine's Day in the year of the Tiger before the Millennium (February 14, 1998 at 11:47 a.m.). My father chose one of the best hospitals in California—Cedars Sinai in Beverly Hills (the Hollywood movie stars' prime choice)—for my mother's labor. The lucky choice of the hospital was because the insurance would cover the costly birth expenses incurred in a place like this with top doctors, prime resources, and "luxury" of all kinds.

At my birth, my mother, like many Chinese, was happy because I was a little tiger (born in the year of tiger) like my father. My father was happy because I was a male born on Valentine's Day, the day of love. Both were blissfully smiling to each other for distinctive reasons.

I am an odd mix and my names show this. For my Chinese passport and my given name, my mother chose "Obedient Tiger" and translated my father's surname from Cavalin to Kai. I ended up being named Kai Hsiao Hu. For my Western name and for my American and Brazilian passports, my father chose Moshe Ben Luiz Cavalin, which in Hebrew means Moses, grandson of Luiz Cavalin. Now, I opt to use the name of **Moshe Kai** because it represents a fusion between the East and the West, the two powerful forces coming together in a mighty roar. My nickname is Shao (Xiao - Little) Hu (Tiger).

My Family

My Father - Vóvó Andradina & Vôvô Luiz passed away before I could know them.

My Mother & Gongon Hsin and Popó Kuei (on my first birthday)

My grandparents lived a harsh life in times of occupation, violence, persecutions, and famine proportioned by wars and hate. The stories recounted to me were of heroic struggle for their continued existence. When I look back to my ancestors, I feel lucky because I do not battle for my survival as they did and I peacefully gather knowledge to help my future.

My father was born in Brasil, an offspring of Italian/Portuguese/Brazilian/German/Polish parents. My mother was born in Taiwan, an offspring of Taiwanese and Mainland Chinese parents. My parents met in Los Angeles. They married, and I was born.

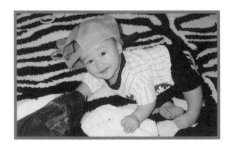

CHAPTER 2:

THE BEGINNING

"A beginning that you make by yourself is the hardest beginning of all." (Yiddish Proverb)

All beginnings are difficult. One has to work hard at the job of learning by himself and persevere to be able to accomplish what he or she has set out to do. One must go over it again and again and be methodic and resilient. If one gives up, one loses.

This book describes my path seeking knowledge, my accomplishments and the little seeds of wisdom that I have gained. I am confident that if somebody traces a plan for themselves it will materialize if a heart is put into it. My father sketched a strategy composed of a mixture of common sense, things that he read and believed, and some things that he conjured himself. Amazingly, the strategy traced worked with extreme success.

THE EARLY YEARS:

FROM BIRTH TO ABOUT EIGHTEEN MONTHS OLD

1 - SENSORIAL STIMULATION

My life from zero through four years old were the most difficult to write. I had to extract the words from my parents with a corkscrew. I interrogated my parents, and I studied intensively my toddler pictures to be able to ask questions and dig up my early years.

My official learning started quickly after my birth. My father thought that it was essential to have in my crib objects that would call my attention and interact with my senses. My crib looked like a carnival, an intense Brazilian one. Many things multicolored were hanging and moving around and above my crib. Classical or soft music was played (barely audible) around me all the time.

Audio/Visual: Sensorial stimulus, in my father's opinion, is an important tool, especially the audio-visual stimulation. The moment that a child is brought from hospital to home, his/her senses should be stirred. Audio and visual stimulation accelerates the infant's brain development.

My father softly played the stereo during most of the day. The chosen music was either classical or easy-listening tunes, especially from the "Rat Pack" -- Dean Martin, Frank Sinatra and Sammy Davis, Jr. Today, I like listening to classics and the music by the "Rat Pack." They are my favorites.

I had a system of bright objects that moved and fluttered around and above my crib directed to my visual search at all time. Later, I had many safe and soft colored toys inside of my crib interacting with my senses.

2 – INTERACTION WITH THE EXTERIOR

I dwelled in an apartment facing a very busy street which produced many unusual noises and disturbances that I grew accustomed to. Those annoying sounds came as hidden blessings. The apartment complex where I lived was in Monterey Park located near the approach pathway for airplanes to LAX (Los Angeles Airport), and close to the Los Angeles Sheriff Headquarters' busy heliport. Most afternoons after work or on his off time, my father would sit outside by the steps facing the street with me on his lap. These moments gave him the opportunity to unwind, have quality time with me, and provide my mother with some rest from my exhaustive daily care. Without knowing, these outside noises gave me a great opportunity to face a mixture of audio and visual stimulus.

I paid attention, very close attention, to what was going on around. Four distinct sounds were present most of the time. The most distinguished was the constant commercial jet planes approaching the LAX. They used to fly around 1000 feet above ground and sometimes these noises were very annoying. For no reason that my father can explain, every time that an airplane would pass over, he would say 'feitchi' (Chinese for airplane) and pointed to the airplane flying above in the sky. He would always make sure that I would see the airplane and that I would hear the word 'feitchi'.

He never expected much from it. After a few months of repetitions like that, when I was just about four months old, I gave him one of the biggest surprises of his life. I pointed up - not directly to the airplane - and mumbled 'fechi', a sound very similar to the real one. My father recognized the connection of the terms and he was very surprised. He ran upstairs to my mother to tell her the news. My mother was skeptical because she believed that my father was out of his mind. My father was not one hundred percent sure either of what he heard. He thought that maybe my mother was right. Less than a few days later, it happened again. This time my father was certain.

Next day, when my father arrived from work, my mother happily told him that when I was on the kitchen table in my small cradle I heard an airplane sound and I muttered 'feichi', which was my own version of the word 'feitchi' and pointed up. She could not believe it either. She called her parents to our home, and they waited anxiously for an airplane to pass by to see my reaction. When this happened, they were dancing and clapping their hands. They were very excited because my first word was in the Chinese idiom.

My mother was a little disappointed. She expected my first word to be 'mama' (mother), but she was still happy for it. From then on, every time I heard a plane, I would mumble the word 'fechi.' If not, my mother would remind me. Popó Chien started to pronounce 'popó' all the time with hopes that I would call her 'grandmother' in the Chinese way very soon (Actually, this was the seventh word I pronounced).

Other sounds always present were from the helicopters. The LA Sheriff Headquarters busy heliport was situated a few blocks away. Each time that a helicopter flew over our house, my father pronounced the word "helicopter". One to two weeks later after I pronounced my first word, when a helicopter was passing by, I pronounced my second "word," something that resembled "cacapoo" and I pointed up somewhere. I repeated this "word" a few times when helicopters went by. It took awhile for my father to understand the connection between the two "words." I replaced the word "helicopter" by the made-up word "cacapoo." Maybe it was easier for me to pronounce it. I do not understand how my brain substituted a sound that was introduced to me by another one that was totally different. I kept using the term "cacapoo" in place of "helicopter" until I was around three years old. Maybe I invented this term because I could not pronounce the English word for helicopter like my father.

"Cacapoo" in our family became the official word for helicopter. Every time a helicopter passed by my parents would say "cacapoo." Even today my parents jokingly call helicopters by the name of "cacapoo." My third word was "mama" and the next was "papa."

The sirens of fire engines and ambulances from the next street fire station were the other sounds always present. It would annoy me very much. Each time that I heard the emergency vehicles sirens, I would cry. My father would cover my ears with his hand and embrace me. Until I was around three years old, I would cry when the emergency vehicles drove near our home and I would run to the bedroom closet or under the bed and try to hide.

Car sounds and blaring horns were abundant in our area. I would stay at the window looking outside to see all the vehicles passing by. I loved to watch buses and trucks drive by our street. My preferred vehicle was the street cleaning truck. When I would hear the street cleaning truck washing and mopping our road, I would run to my favorite kitchen chair and look out the window at that marvelous contraption. The windows of our apartment were locked most of the time because my parents were afraid that I might fall. This precaution made the California summers hotter in our apartment.

Snoozing by my favorite window

3 – HOME STRUCTURE

When I was about three months old, my Popó Kuei started to share a great part of my life by babysitting me almost daily. She could not keep up with me though. Once I started crawling, I crawled everywhere, pulling down drapes, towels, etc. I liked to push things down that were within my reach. My mother was afraid that I was going to get hurt and that my grandmother would not be able to handle me. My father, who usually acted in response to any of my mother's prompts, constructed a square fenced area made of plastic, cardboard, and tape.

The "Play Area"

About this time, my father bought me a myriad of safe toys, especially plastic animals, little houses, cars, and picture books and placed them inside of this "play area." He would spend most of his free time inside, engaging in games and playing with me. I do not remember any of these events but I believe that it would be very amusing to me to see my father playing with my toys and teddy bears.

This spacious fenced area was build to enable me to be near to my family all the time where I could see the kitchen and the living room well. Those were the rooms where my family spent most of their days either working or taking ease. I was secure and I would not make any trouble. I could play with my toys and watch them doing their chores. The interaction and the learning were constant. I usually would stand up, looking over the fence to see what my family was doing. During the instruction time, my parents would come inside the fence to interact with me. The "play area" stayed up about six months. It was taken apart when I was a little over eight months old after I learned how to jump over the fence and free to "raise hell."

4 – INTERACTION WITH THE SURROUNDINGS

"The dynamic interplay between progressive and regressive events results in relatively rapid brain growth in the first two years of life, by which time it has achieved near 80% of its adult weight. By the age of 5 years, the size of the child's brain is approximately 90% of adult size". [1] In other words, our brains are open for learning and interaction at a very early age.

Children are canvassing their surroundings to probe, interact, and analyze inputs for survival purposes. This is an innate animal instinct. A two year old child has an open intellect to get acquainted with the environment. This condition can be explored almost with no limits by introducing select learning tools. I believe this is very crucial. This age is a very important period in which parents and children should interrelate and work together. Parents should allocate their time for their children's learning.

My parents did not have experience in rearing a child. Their realization that I could put together sound, visuals, and words was very surprising. They felt compelled to do something about my learning and development. My father started to put different educational ideas into practice.

First Birthday   **'Horsing' Around**

FROM CRIB TO ABOUT THREE YEARS OLD

5 – THE CARDS: A GIANT STEP

Shortly after my first four words, my father realized that I was able to react to visual and audio stimulus. The interaction of a common object that the child can relate (like a bottle, a toy, their mouth, etc) in their daily life, plus the visual (show the object and the spelling), the audio (read its name, make its corresponding sound) will produce a response from any child. These interactions repeated many times and consistently will bring --without any doubts-- a positive learning experience and a new understanding of the environment to the child.

My father with his unconventional ideas about early education put forth a project to educate me. His experience in animation and graphics gave him the inspiration to start making some cards showing pictures, words, and sound effects by reading the words and making sounds. In his opinion, the main point of this type of instruction was to attract mine attention and set in motion an interaction between me and the object shown.

According to him, this early age is a very important time to interact with a child with love and to dedicate all spare time to their learning. Verbalizing any object or action when used around the children is very important. They associate the words quickly with the actions and objects used daily.

Shortly after I mastered the words "feitchi" and "cacapoo," my father created four cards (airplane- feitchi, helicopter - cacapoo, mama, and papa) adding their pictures and their spelling in large letters on a half page cards (On appendix 1, it is shown an example of the cards used.) My father chose feitchi (in Chinese) for airplane and "cacapoo" for helicopter because I already interacted well with these words and the objects described.

Another reason was that my father wanted to know if I could translate the graphic words to the sound that I already knew. Big surprise: The first time I set my eyes on the card, I said the corresponding words. The other two cards had the spellings of "papa" and "mama" with their pictures. It was a no-brainer. Quickly, I was able to differentiate between the two and would "read" the card and say the corresponding words. Also, when my father or my mother would come to me, they would say either papa or mama and I would usually repeat back to them. My father was amazed when I pronounced the word "feichi" on the first time that he showed me the airplane card. He wondered how I could deduct somehow that the airplane on the card corresponded with the airplane seen in the sky.

With the success of the first set of cards, my father expanded the cards to eleven. He created seven more picture and text cards: Tiger, bottle, mouth, eyes, nose, hand, and foot. He chose tiger because that was part of my name. My father added the bottle card because this was an object that he interacted with me during the constant feeding. "Bottle" was the only word with no sound but my parents showed the card with the "bottle" many times and at the feeding time they showed the real bottle repeating the word "bottle".

After spending many hours showing the cards, and interacting with me with no success, I finally pronounced the word "botte" when my mother was holding a bottle in her hand and preparing to feed me. I would say: "botte" always because I did not pronounce the letter "l" well. It was clear, though, that I was referring to a bottle. Another strange occurrence was that I started to say "botte" when I wanted to be fed. My parents noticed that I would go into a frenzy saying many times the word "botte" when I would see my mother approaching me with a bottle in her hand. It also seemed that I interacted well with the picture or the object shown in the cards.

Sometimes I tried to imitate their actions; that is, I would touch my mouth with my finger imitating my parents when they showed me the "mouth" card. My parents would point to a card and they would point and touch their body parts and then do the same to me. Not more than a few weeks later, I knew and pronounced in a sequence something close to the words: nose, mouth, tiger, and eyes. These positive interactions stimulated the learning process. I still wonder how a baby can conclude by seeing an eye in somebody's face that he would also have an eye on his own face.

My parents spent most of their free time showing the picture in the cards, pronouncing the corresponding words and sounds. "Nose" and "eyes" did not have corresponding sounds, hence my father created something to interact like pointing to them, blinking the eyes, or bending the nose with his fingers. He created a new card each time I conquered the previous one. My parents usually would start a new card doing three steps with it: They put their hands to hide the images and they would show the word and pronounce them a few times. In the beginning, my reaction to the graphic letters was slow. Next, they would show the images with the word and reinforce the verbalization.

After some time, I would pronounce the word just by seeing the letters. I appreciate all my parents' demanding efforts to educate me.

The process of mastering each card seemed to my father to take much time. He persisted though. Each time that I mastered a card, my father would create a new one. Before I was seven months old, I could recognize twenty-one objects and pronounce their names when shown only the words on the cards.

My parents were amazed that I would say the word on the card without seeing the pictures. I could "read the card." For example, they showed me the spelling of the word "tiger" on the card, and I would say "tiger" and try to imitate the tiger's roar without seeing the tiger's image. My mother would pronounce words like "bottle" or "bath" in the moment which she would bottle feed me or give me a bath. After a while, when my mother would say the world bottle, I would smile and do joyful movements of a happy baby. When she would say the word "bath", I would immediately cry. My father thought it was funny that I cried when she would say the word "bath" and I would stop crying when my mother would say the word "bottle". It was like a switch button that turns on and off my emotions. My mother decided not to use the word "bath" anymore because she felt that she was hurting me by making me cry. From then on, she would surprise me with the bath (I would cry each time she bathed me). In my early days, it seems to me that I really hated the water. Now, I love water so much that one of my favorite sports is scuba diving.

Another word that I did not like was "fire engine." The fire engines would race through my street all the time because the fire station was located near my apartment complex. Each time one approached with the siren on, I would cry. And each time my father would show me the fire engine card and make its sound, I would cry. Finally, he stopped showing me the "fire engine" card. Sirens and high pitched noises bother me to this day.

6 – CONSTRUCTING SENTENCES

At this point, my parents started to emphasize the written word. They hid the picture with one hand and then they would read the word a few times, showing only the letters in the pictures. After awhile, they were surprised when I would be spelling without the pictures. I could "read the card"!!! For example, when I was shown the graphics of the word "mouth", I would mumble "mouth" and I would bring my hand (sometimes my foot) to my mouth and touch it. They were not certain if I recognized the letters as a phrase or if I reacted to the graphic of the letters as a picture.

When I was about seven months old, my father started to construct sentences and phrases like "clap hands," "get tiger," "touch nose." He would then read and do the actions mentioned and help me mimic his gestures. It took a little time before I was able to "read" and imitate those simple actions when prompted by the cards or using words. After a while when my father showed me the "tiger" card, I would start to look for one of my tiger toys and then grab it. This positive feedback showed my parents that they were on the right educational fast track.

7 – COMPUTER

After I was two years old, my father recreated and added cards into a CD, including on it real sounds and animations. I started to be acquainted with the computer. When I was almost four years old, he started to teach me the use of the computer.

When a child is eighteen months old, he or she already has an open intellect for learning and we should explore this condition endlessly. My parents expanded my horizons to Math when I was barely two years old. My mother started showing one object then showing two of the same, saying the words one and then two. She told me that it was a frustrating task, especially because she did not feel that I understood the adding notion. The breakthrough came when she showed me two small cars and I said two "car" and showed two fingers imitating my mother. She showed two plastic tigers and I said "two tiger." I didn't know how to pluralize the subject yet, but the notion of "two objects" was mastered. My mother was ecstatic. She started expanding the addition tasks and introduced me to subtraction. She would tutor two to five sections of thirty minutes to one hour in different parts of the day with breaks in between sections. She would divide this leaning time for Math and Reading.

The Super Hero

Super Heroes become tired too, what do you expect?

13

When I was four years old, my parents started to design a learning system. They came up with the M³R system (3M's: Math, Music, and Martial Arts plus Reading) which became a significant part of my learning strategy. Another important aspect of learning was repeating the exercises until I conquered its meaning and its implications before we went on to a new exercise. Practice well is essential. Speed is not.

8 – THE M³R (Math, Music, Martial Arts and Reading).

Music and Language (Math is a language) stimulate the right and left parts of the brain. My mother worked with me on Math and Reading. My father would work with me on Math/ Martial Arts/ Physical activities, plus he hired a teacher for music. I loved to study under my mother because she would teach me with games and she had a great deal of patience. I loved to spend learning time with her and I would look forward every day for her tutoring. Martial Arts and Physical activities with my father were kind of rough. As I see now, Martial Arts gave me discipline and dedication, and Music with Mrs. Fujimoto gave me a paradise.

A - MATHEMATICS

Ever since I can remember, my parents stressed Math. When I was four years old, I had already mastered addition, and I was progressing well in subtraction. At that time, everything intensified because my father came up with the idea that I should utilize both sides of the brain extensively, especially the right side. He placed emphasis in Math, adding a few hours in the daily study routine.

According to many studies, the right brain deals with novel situations and new environmental conditions. My father wanted to develop the right brain by engaging it with math. Another important aspect is that the left brain deals with routine and it stores and processes procedures and algorithms. The true learning happens when the knowledge and skills are transferred from the right to left brain, i.e. the novel is "routinized." [2]

Math is the gateway to all the science in the brain because it develops the 'Broca region'. [3] By an individual's intense use of this area, the mathematical calculations can be expanded permanently to the area of the brain that coordinates the eyes movements, which would increase the speed and analysis of the individual's computation and reasoning.

Before I reached five years old, I was using seventh grade math books used in middle schools. My father started to teach me to use more complex computers applications around this time.

Proudly showing my homework

B – MUSIC: PIANO

Music is processed by both the left and the right sides of the brain. [4] We are open to our perception and audio stimulation of what is going on around us as it propitiates the learning of any instrument, music or language spoken, around an infant. Before the age of twelve, it is the ideal time for a kid to put emphasis in the learning of his native language and to initiate the learning of another language in order to expand their horizon. Music is important because it develops and stimulates the use of both lobes of the brain as well as improves the alpha state, which is the tranquil meditative condition that produces a refuge from stress and the worries of the day.

Piano was introduced to me when I was four years old. Ms. Fujimoto, a piano teacher, offered to teach my father piano; meanwhile, he would teach her computers. My father said, "How about my son?" She inquired my age and then said: "Four year old children's attention span is very low but I will try anyway." Probably, a forty minute of focus and concentration for a piano session was undemanding because I was already used to the daily home study sections structured by my parents. I did okay on the first half hour class trial and I was set up for a weekly class.

To find a great piano teacher willing to teach a four-year old was near a miracle. This worked well because I was able to focus my attention on the piano during the weekly forty minutes piano session. Not having much money, my father bought a keyboard for my home exercises. When I became five years old, I extended the piano session to one hour and a half and then to two hours per week. I was blessed; my piano teacher was a very endearing and gracious lady and, above all, a master pianist.

Mrs. Fujimoto   **Practicing**   **Senior Home Demo**

At home, I had a keyboard. I really treasured playing the keyboard because my Popó Kuei took me to different senior and convalescent homes to play. I loved to entertain and bring many smiles to suffering people. Popó Kuei proudly would take me to different places to perform. We would travel by bus and we would have fun visiting and roaming through the neighborhood. Many city bus drivers came to know us well and when they would spot us they would stop the bus just to pick us up.

C – MARTIAL ARTS

Physical training is very good to build up and maintain good health and physical conditioning Martial Arts as physical training is better because it develops personal autonomy, courage, self-reliance, speed, endurance and strength. When I was four years old, I learned horseback riding and started practicing this sport seriously most of the weekends during my fourth and fifth years. When I was four, my father also designed a physical training routine for me. During the weekends, my parents and I would take long walks, but usually my father would end up carrying me. During the week, we would walk around a few blocks after dinner.

Judo/Jiujitsu **Karate** **Horseback Riding**

With the M³R development, I was introduced to Martial Arts. I started training judo, jiujitsu and karate with my father two to three times a week. I had many shortcomings. It was kind of a bumpy beginning: Brazilian jiujitsu is a rough sport and for judo, I needed a partner of my size. My father was afraid to teach me chokes and arm locks because I could harm another kid when playing with them. I went to a judo academy, but the training problem was not solved. I did not have partners my size. I was too small compared to the other students and my only partner was a two years older chubby kid and the training of shoulder throws was excruciating to me. We did not have technique and I always ended up on the floor being dominated by brutal force. So, my father took me out of the dojo and started teaching me only karate, and judo rolls. He emphasized walking to build up my endurance.

At this point, I did not like to practice my father's martial arts. I was not strong enough to deal with bigger kids in judo, Brazilian jiu-jitsu was too violent and I did not like to take the long walks. Karate was OK. When I saw some kids practicing Wushu in the park, I loved it and found a way to escape my father's training. He agreed with my choice. Afraid that I would start training too young without his protection, my father promised to let me start Wushu when I was 6 years old. What gave me impetus to train hard in the park was what my father told me: "If you do not put your heart in it, you will come back training with me." That was great encouragement to do my best. When I started to gain many gold and silver trophies, my father was beaming all the time and the threat dissipated.

Goodbye Judo, Brazilian Jiujitsu and Horseback Riding and Hello Wushu.

D – READING

At the start of my education, my mother used very easy books, read stories, and used my father's sentence cards. She structured two to four sections of thirty minutes to one hour throughout different parts of the day.

When she got her MBA, she started dedicating more of her time to me. When I was two years old, my father took another job to supplement our family income and my mother became my sole reading instructor. The next step after I graduated "reading" cards, my mother would go often to bookstores looking to buy used toddlers' books (the new ones were too expensive). I was able to read easy books before I was three years old.

To pursue the M³R fully, my parents went to different schools to see which materials and books were used for the kindergarten, first, and second grades. They chose the books that were universally used in the elementary schools and the ones that they liked. The instruction became five hours a day minimum. After a while, my mother started to visit the best elementary schools to see which books they used for classes and then acquire them. This is what I call the start of my "formal education."

As I advanced, reading, grammar, and vocabulary were more oriented toward sciences, facts and people that changed the world.

I would try to read wherever and whatever I could.

THE LEARNING YEARS:
SIX YEARS OLD TO ABOUT SEVEN YEARS OLD

In my opinion, the ages of three to seven are the most important to develop children's behavior and their brain patterns. Parents' full participation at this time in their children's lives is behavior conditioning and essential for their future.

Just after my 6th birthday, I began my training in Chinese Martial Arts. My mother became my designated driver and companion to my Wushu classes. Goodbye walking, horseback riding, karate, jiujitsu, and judo; Hello Wushu!

When I became six years old, it was time for me go to school. I went to an interview with the administrator of a public elementary school. My parents knew that I was well ahead in academics than the other students my age, and they tried to place me in a more advanced grade. The principal told me the only choice was that I had to start in the 1st grade. My father could not see me going back to study things that I already knew well. Starting 1st. grade would make me go back at least five school years. The school administration wanted me to revisit what I learned all over again. No way, I was not willing to do that.

My father took me to private elementary/middle schools. On my first try, after I showed my advanced algebra book (1st. year college book) that I was studying to the interviewing teacher, she said that she did not know math as much as I did. I was amazed by the statement. We went to another private middle school, and they were willing to accept me there as a fourth grader. My designated future teacher took me to a room and tested me. I showed my books that I was studying, and she told me that I was at the level of an eighth/ninth grader in some subjects (English especially) and college level in others (like in Math). She went to talk to the principal. The principal came to my father and told him that she could not accept me because the difference of knowledge and age. She concluded that I would be a focus of disturbance to older students. My father already was reluctant to take me to a private school because it was expensive and this refusal made him reject thoughts about private school.

I did not have any place to go, and my parents needed to decide what to do. They determined that I would start home schooling. It was a hard choice.

My mother was forced to quit her part-time job and start teaching me fulltime. This made us poorer, but it put me well ahead of the regular students. Many things that we think are bad and may lead us to suffering will perhaps transform into a great blessing. Our lives changed, we needed to count our pennies as our finances diminished. We suffered due to this decision, but our family structure became stronger and my schooling progressed faster with dedicated parents who turned into devoted tutors. When I was seven years old, I dominated Advanced Algebra and started working on Pre-Calculus. My English and Science comprehension were not so advanced, but I was still a few years ahead of my peers.

Comparing my speed of learning to a regular elementary/ middle/high school student, I can see the mistake many parents make when they let the schools provide all the learning and education to their children. Parents stop educating and guiding their children, thinking that all is OK until it is too late. I believe this is wrong. Parents need to contribute in the education of their children more than any outside influential force in their formative years (especially to counterbalance liberal teachings).

In the U.S., many of the public schools operate at the speed of the slowest students, which my parents and I do not agree. The money for education and teachers' salary is dismal. Many qualified teachers seek other careers. Many school programs have subjects that are classified as general education which truly are really misplaced, lame propositions. In other words, they are a waste of time. We are losing the solid American educational nature to a complacent one and turning our education into a broken system. We're slowly losing the competitive nature in schools and becoming too "soft" and complacent. In the past, U.S. was number one in education in the developed countries. More recently, the U.S. was classified 14th for reading, 17th for sciences and 25th for math out of 34 OECD countries!!! [7]

What shocks me the most is the spread of liberal ideas on sex and disparate behavior taught an accepted in place of the curriculum subjects that should be the sole object of learning. During the class, I don't care to hear about a teacher's opinion about his/her sexual life, beliefs on abortion, homosexuality or anything else that doesn't have to do with the subject in the curriculum. It is my belief that this is completely out of order. We need to be aware of liberal teachers and challenge their teachings early on. The lobbyists in D.C. have agendas and want their ideas expressed in textbooks.

Indoctrination of wrong ideals and ideas, misplaced political correctness and political agendas are "dumbing" our system down and with that the students descend into a downward spiral, lacking critical thinking skills. Character formation and citizenship should be a strict parent's work. A bad apple can destroy an entire basket.

9 – SCHOOL BOOKS

For each book that I finished, my parents would buy another one more advanced. Emphasis was placed on Sciences and Math books.

Home Schooling

SEVEN YEARS OLD TO ABOUT NINE YEARS OLD

The Intense years

These three years were very intense. Many triumphs were on my plate. I couldn't stop. Blessed be the Almighty. I succeeded well with things that occupied my time: Martial Arts, Piano, Play Productions, School, College, and Sports.

My family has a custom that prior to every birthday I may ask for any gift I choose: an event to see, a place to go, a long trip or a particular gift. A few days before I was seven years old, I asked my father, as my birthday gift, to participate at the Pomona International Martial Arts competition because I wanted a trophy. My father was very surprised and worried but he granted my wish. I did not train for the competitions, but I put all my heart into the contest. Four days after my seventh birthday, I participated in three events in the Martial Arts Compete International – Pomona, California and I won my first three trophies: One in Wushu (gold), one in Choi La Fut Kwan (silver - staff) and one in Kung Fu (silver).

My achievement emboldened my father to let me compete whatever place I would choose. In those three years, I was very successful in Martial Arts. I entered in many local competitions (all gold or silver) and I participated on thirty-seven top national and international competitions, and I got twenty-six gold and nine silver medals. I won gold and two silver medals in the U.S. World Championship in Karate, and I won three National Championships in three consecutive years in Wushu/Kung Fu competitions. I traveled around different states to compete. It was very exciting.

Competitions & Trophies

My first trophies & Sifu Nan Li

MARTIAL ARTS SIFUS

Competition Sifus: Sifu Sha (Wushu) and Sifu Yudeng (Gun-Fu).

ELAC Sifu Wu (Weapons), UCLA Sifus Tsou and Schonfeld (Tai Chi)

I am very good in Karate, but I love the Chinese Wushu more, even though it is more difficult. The difference is that Karate is a straight form; Wushu is a round form and more complex and more difficult to learn but a more powerful style. To be good at it, one needs to train thrice as hard to develop gymnastics and fighting skills. In my opinion, there are four fighting styles that are superior to all others: Brazilian Jiu-jitsu, Muay Thai, Kung Fu and Wushu. The Wushu develops the ability to fly and hit the target. It interests me, but this ability declines in older ages. Also, I train Kung Fu for my older days when my physical conditions make harder to use my acrobatic Wushu to implement the flying kicks. In the future, I hope to learn Muay Thai and Brazilian Jiu-jitsu. A man that knows well these four Martial Arts will be an all around Martial Artist. This is my goal. Bruce Lee's Jeet Kune Do is a mix of different Martial Arts.

Piano/Plays

I love piano and arts in general. I was progressing well in piano and Chinese arts. I was invited to perform in many piano recitals and plays, but my father prioritized Academics and Martial Arts. He declined many invitations that had to do with anything else, including "The Oprah Show," the most viewed daytime show in US television. I could not take away my time and efforts from my goals. I am proud that I played piano in a recital in Gardena with famous artists in honor of my piano teacher, Mrs. Fujimoto. I played piano and performed in many other places.

Gardena Recital in Honor of Ms. Fujimoto with many famous musicians

Ms. Fujimoto   &   Many Piano Recitals

Members of the **Los Angeles Asian Arts Talents Foundation** under Donna Cheng invited me to participate in two dance competitions and a dance festival in California. I sweated a lot, but all went well. Also, I was invited by the AATF to be in the "Monkey King" play for the American-Chinese Dance Association. My surprise was that I was chosen to the important part of Monkey King's helper. My success in this play brought me an invitation to play the principal part in another play, the Monkey King's *The Journey to the West* for the AATF/ACDA.

The Dance Competitions & More Trophies

The Journey to West and the Monkey King

25

Parades

Demos: Rosemead, Palisades and San Diego

Eagle Form   **Lion Dance**

Invited to Demo with visiting Hunan Martial Monks.

San Diego, CA   Trophies   Irvine, CA

"The USA International Chinese Talent Arts Association," through their president, Master Zhen Ping Lu, gave me the honor of inviting me to become a member. I became the youngest member of the USA ICTAA at the age of eight years old. I also performed many times for charity, senior and convalescent homes for the USA ICTAA which made me very happy. To put good spirits in a person that is suffering and make them momentarily forget their pain is a great gift, but it is a greater gift to the soul for one that cheers the one that suffers.

Senior Home Demos

Academically, I was in limbo. At six and at seven years old, I attempted to enter different public and private schools. I was being home schooled because no elementary/middle/high school would accept me on my terms. Each school gave some odd reasons not to accept me: I was too young to take a class with classmates much older than I or I was too advanced for them; I would make them feel inferior to have a bright younger kid in their midst; they would bully me; and in general, school officials gave me the idea that I would be a disturbing factor to older students or too much trouble. My father was not very upset with their refusal. Many Californian schools are very liberal and operate at the speed of the slowest student in the class and the learning process becomes sluggish. Some teachers do not challenge students because it is troublesome. To challenge a bright student it would cause more effort on the teachers' part. Human nature is to take the easiest path to laziness. The education becomes soft and condescending with no challenges

One day, after many refusals, my father had an inspiration. We went to Los Angeles City College, a junior college, asking them if I could take some math classes. The Dean of Mathematics was all for it, but the Dean of Academics said no. **His words**: no test, no interview for this kid or any other seven year-old kid. My age hindered his vision. He saw the envelope but not its content. School bureaucrats, self-called educators, can be so blind. I learned later that this Dean is now the vice-president of a Los Angeles Community College!!! This is what I mean when I say one should not believe in school pen pushers. They only see their nose in front of their face, if even that. My parents were sad to see me rejected so many times. I was rejected for being advanced in my studies!!! What a puzzling world.

There are two types of colleges in the U. S. (besides Trade colleges): junior colleges and universities. Junior colleges are the first two years of university and once one graduates from a junior college one is able to transfer to a third year of an university and complete the last two years for a Bachelor's degree. Junior colleges give A.A. degrees and the universities give Bachelor degrees. Many students go through the junior college route first and university later because junior colleges are less expensive. My parents did not have the means, so they decided to put me in a junior college to cut down the expenses.

I went back to the drawing board. I was stressed. I wanted to study, and I wanted to progress. My parents gave me all their support for me to learn at home and go forward. I wanted to enter a university, but the cost, the paperwork, and bureaucracy impeded me. My parents were set with the idea to put me in a college as soon as possible. One year later we tried again to enter in yet another junior college. Our perseverance struck gold. The V.P. of Academics, Dr. Moyer, thinking outside the box, let me take the assessment test. The two most important exams were Math and English. In math, there were three levels on the test. 44 students were taking exam at that time I took it. 41 students took "Level One Test." 3 students, including myself, took "Level Two Test." Without knowing their grades, it means that I scored above 41 of the 44 high school graduates taking the examination. They were at least ten years older than I. In English, my most challenging subject, I was just on the same level as the average high school graduate, which was a low average, and I was not very proud.

A funny thing occurred before the exam. My father and I (I was eight years old at that time) walked into the classroom for the entrance test. The examiner told my father that I could not come inside of the classroom; I needed to wait outside. Only the people taking the test were allowed inside. My father told the tester that I was the one taking the exam. The examiner thought that it was a joke and smiled. When my father went out of the room and left me there, they started realizing that I was the one for the test. They asked for my identification and all the examiners came to look at it as if my ID was forged or I was something out of this world. Later, before the exam, they started asking the students what math level test they wanted to take. The majority asked for level one. When they came to me, I asked for level two (I wanted to take level three, but I took level two under my father's strict orders). About that time, the students were looking at me with disbelief, and they started murmuring. I felt like a planetary alien.

I passed the exam, and I was accepted to take classes conditionally depending on my behavior and grades, but there was a big hold up: I was authorized only to take a maximum of six units. I chose my two strong points: Mathematics and Martial Arts. The ball was put in my hands, and I darted with it. My hands were a little bit tied but, finally, I was in college.

My first day in college

September 5, 2006 was my first day of college. I was barely eight years old. To my surprise, I made history for being the youngest student to take college classes in the US ever. Mr. Michael Kearney – now 27 – was the only other student to enter college at my age. He was one week older than I when he entered the University of South Alabama. After two and a half short years of college, he got his bachelor's degree in Anthropology at the age of ten. He is the youngest student to get a bachelor's degree ever. Amazing!!! (I guess his brain was fueled with a lot of southern corn and grits.)

Two things slowed me down though. First, I was authorized only to be part-time as a conditional student (K-12). Second, my father did not let me take the Math classes at my level. He wanted me to take College Intermediate Algebra as my first course. He wanted me to improve on what I learned at home but, more importantly, to make one hundred percent sure that I would get only A's to show the administration and the disbelievers that I had what it takes. My father was right. Taking a lower Math course and Martial Arts as Physical Education, I did not need to study hard (but I did anyway), and I had more time to dedicate to other endeavors especially Kung-Fu and Karate competitions.

Sophia: (Physics)   **Claudia and Jozette: (Math)**   **Yesenia: (English)**

Big brothers – College: Yemin, Lin and Kerry
Shaolin: Guang, Liang, Xiaolong, Yudeng and Guangyun

Alyson - Scuba partner.

Martial Arts Class. Prof. Judge and Dr. Moyer,
two of the most outstanding educators at ELAC.

CHAPTER 3:

THE LEARNING STRATEGY AND TACTICS

Strategy is a plan of action to accomplish a specific goal reaching out into the future. Tactics are small shorter term plans within the strategy to accomplish a much broader strategic goal.

"Strategy requires thought, tactics require observation." **Max Euwe (Dutch chess Grandmaster, mathematician, and author).**

"Strategy without tactics is the slowest route to victory. Tactics without strategy is the noise before defeat." **Sun Tzu (Chinese military general, strategist, philosopher, and author)**

This book describes my path seeking knowledge, my accomplishments and some of the little wisdom that I have. I am confident that if somebody traces a plan for themselves it will work if a heart is put on it. Amazingly, my father's implemented strategy worked with extreme success.

I was blessed. My first two professors, Sifu Dr. Wu and Laosu Liao, were truly masters. They illuminated my daily college maze with knowledge and wisdom. They were of Chinese background and they took me under their wings. It was a perfect start.

All my first professors during my college span acted in a peculiar way. In the first two to three weeks, they looked at me doubtfully throwing a barrage of questions to test my behavior and my knowledge on class subjects. On my part, I used reverse psychology. I always sat in front of the class facing the teacher to mark my presence in an open challenge with no fear. Any question posed to the class, I tried to be the first to answer. I was always prepared. I had done my homework and much more. If the professor asked the class to do five problems, I did fifteen. If the professor asked the students to do the odd problems, I did all the evens and odds. My tactics were to win by overwhelming the adversary and I won big time. By the end of the semester, they would realize that I was a good student and worked hard to grasp the subject at hand.

The majority of my professors treated me well and they became my friends. Most of my professors came to my piano recitals and to my commencement. Now, I can walk freely to their office and they treat me like their peer. I have a great rapport with them and a mutual trust. Some professors think that I know it all and I wish that would be true but sadly I know the very little that I know.

From this rapport, they came to trust my work more than I merited. During my two years plus in the college, I remember two incidents involving me. The first – I had been answering around 80% of the professor's questions in a physics class. At one point, before the professor posed a new question he said to the students: "This question is for all of you except Mr. Moshe. We have been in this class for two months now, and he is the only one that answers my questions, and he does it correctly. Now it is time for you to follow his example." I became red in the face and felt a little embarrassed but proud for being recognized.

The second incident was when a math professor that said: "The question that I will put to the class only Mr. Moshe and I know the answer to it, and I would like somebody else to answer." He posed the question and nobody in the class knew the response. I could hear the crickets and birds chirping. After a few seconds, he turned to me and asked me the same question theatrically, slowly and aloud. I was nervous, sweating nails. I did not want to let my professor down. By miracle, I was able to answer correctly the question asked. A day prior, by luck, the hard worker's luck, I went over this very tricky math problem, and I was not very sure of the solution. At the end of the class, I told the teacher that it would be embarrassing for both of us if I would not know the answer. He turned to me smiling and told me that he trusted my knowledge. I am always scared when somebody thinks that I know all (or any) answers because I know that I know little.

My first year (two semesters) and the 12 units in college were a stroll in the park. It was kind of easy, and it gave me more time to solve the college maze. My age, my straight A's performance, and being on the Dean's Honor

List made me well known on the campus. Seeing that, the V.P. of Academics, Dr. Moyer, decided to let me take as many units as I wanted, and with this action he opened the college doors for me: I became a full fledge student. I could take as many classes I wanted and choose the subjects which I wanted. In my book, he is my hero. A good feeling of accomplishment entered my soul and I flew into the Academic "heavens" by getting A+s in all subjects

I look at my undertakings unlike most people. The success is due not to me. My professors, my home schooling, and my parents' dedication did the feat. My merit was to strictly follow my parents' guidance with my whole heart and listen to my professors with full attention. They deserve the glory, if there is any, because they gave me this great opportunity in my life. The professors give the gift of knowledge, second only to the gift of love from our parents, and they should be considered our good friends. We, as students, need to seize all learning chances that we can. Once the opportunity passes by us, we cannot catch them anymore. It is gone. End of the game!! Ask any wise elder person about it.

During each college semester, if one gets A's in all subjects taken (if more than 6 units), one enters the Dean's Honor List. Three consecutive times on the Dean's List, one receives a President's Award. I have been on the Dean's Honor List, and I received all the college President's Award during my time at ELAC. In the spring of 2007, I was the youngest student ever to be on the Dean's Honor List in any college in the U.S. In the fall of 2007, I was the youngest student ever to receive a President's Award in any college in the U.S.

Big Brother Alex

What I like the most in my classes is that I made friends who turned out to be like big brothers. Some of my best friends, Alex, Alfredo, Rafael and Armando, have been with me for the last two years through many of my college classes. Alex, Rafael and I transferred together to UCLA continuing our friendship.

The most important point of my success is that I always study ahead the school material. For example, if the next quarter I will take Differential Geometry or Complex Analysis as my subject, I will study at least two months before class. When the time comes to take it, I will already know much of the subject. I will also know my weak points and what to ask and explore with the new professor.

MARTIAL ARTS VIPs

Grand Master Ming Lum   **Shaolin Master Shi De Cheng**

Receiving the USA World Champion Award from Don the Dragon Wilson; Tsang (Chi Wai)

GK Cheung   **Shin Koyamada**   **Robin Shou**

COMING OF AGE (10 thru 12)

Forever missing you

My 10th. year on this earth was a very sad and dark one. I witnessed my Popó Kuei, being crushed under the wheels of a bus. I miss her very much because she was my babysitter, my friend, my biggest fan, my companion in my adventures and now my angel robbed away from me by a bus driver. Each time I remember it, my soul cries aloud. I understand that this was HIS wish and I bow to HIM. There is nothing I can do about it. I need to be strong and resilient. I would exchange all my achievements for my grandmother to come back even for a day. The ones that have their grandparents as companions until a late age are the lucky ones.

With her death, it looked like the sky came down on me. In this tragic year, I had more bad news. Without Popó Kuei, my mother was forced to work more to take care of me curtailing much of her time. My afternoon trips with my grandmother ceased. My father became sick and could not produce as much money to take care of us as usual, and I was forced to quit my piano classes and cancel my martial arts competitions for lack of funds. It hurts: No more trips or Martial Arts competitions. Bad things were happening around me, and I was pushed to understand that to be successful I needed to be strong, resilient, and tough.

In this terrible year, I was a college sophomore (2nd. year of university) and the Associate Press (an international news agency) published an article about me. I became well known overnight. Google and Yahoo published more than one million articles worldwide about my accomplishment and it was followed by hundreds of TV stations in the world. I gave many interviews to TVs, Newspapers and participated in several TV Shows.

I was surprised by the fame, but I could not be happy. Again, I would exchange all that for my grandmother coming back even for a day. I remember that she would give me a wonderful smile and a hug for each "A" that I received. I became stronger, striving for all A+'s to be able to see in the eyes of my mind the picture of my grandmother hugging and smiling at me.

I was chosen the best of the best in Martial Arts by Tiger Claw. (Photos by John Nguyen)

My 11[th.] year was a political year. I decided to run for the ELAC Students Union Presidency at my college. The Associate Dean of Students Activities, the woman in charge of the elections, did all in her power to defeat my candidacy because she felt that I could not represent the students well because of my age. I became the administration's enemy. In June 2009, I graduated, but I was not recognized by the ELAC administration. Out of the $175,000 in scholarships the V. P. of Students Services gave me not a penny. I was blacklisted. They forbid me to use MESA resources even though I was a Math student. They did not put my name as Summa Cum Laude in the Commencement booklet.

Merit does not count in the V.P. of Students Services' calendar even though I graduated with a GPA of 4.0 (All A's) and no other student did better than I in the graduating class of 2009. Many told me that I should have played ball with him and the ADSS during the ASU elections. I sincerely

36

believe that if one conducts correctly and does good deeds some doors will close, and those that are closed are the ones you do not want to go inside. Maybe the doors are attractive, but they are the ones that end eating up the soul of the ones that enter it.

I was not recognized inside of the ELAC administration, and it seems that the only administrator that liked me was the V. P. of Academics, the great Dr. Moyer. The professors and the Labs personnel were the ones that kept the educational ship afloat and all of them that I had the honor to be their student were very competent. I was blessed. In all the classes that I have chosen, it seems that I would choose the best professor around. Many of them became my friends for life. I was not sad by the pen pushers' attitude because I knew that I was correct. As soon as I graduated, many doors opened for me. I was recognized outside of the college spheres above all my dreams. I received certificates of recognition from the high echelons in the city, state and national government.

City of Monterey Park Certificate of Recognition – Given by councilman David Lau.
Letter of Recognition – California Governor Arnold Schwarzenegger.

Certificate of Recognition by the California Senate.
Letter of Recognition from Senator Gloria Romero.
Certificate of Congressional Recognition - U.S. Congress
'Youngest student to hold an A.A. Degree in the U.S.'

I was forced to stop and not transfer to a four year university when I was eleven for lack of funds. Many told me to transfer right away so that would assure me to be the second student ever to get a Bachelors degree from a university at the age of 12 years old.

I am not here on this earth to set records or compete with others. I do not want to be better or like anybody else. I want to be a better person, a better 'me'. When one tries to be somebody else, he loses himself which is very precious.

LA Sheriff Leroy David Baca conferred me with the Sheriff Star.
Master Zhen Ping Lu, head of the USA ICTAA, accepted me as its youngest members.

Sincerely, I believed that I could pass college with good grades and at the same time train hard for martial arts competitions. My father said that the lack of money was a blessing in disguise. He believed that I needed to get a scholarship to be able to enter the top USA universities and the only way was if I graduated Summa Cum Laude. My father's advice was valuable. I received the A.A. degree with the highest honors on June 06, 2009 and I became the youngest student in the USA to get an A.A. Degree Summa Cum Laude at the age of 11.

After I got my A.A. Degree, I went in a short phase of despair. I did not receive any scholarships. The universities in the U.S. are very expensive. Although I applied only to two universities, I quickly realized that my parents could not afford to move and pay for the expenses involved and I didn't receive any scholarship. I was forced to stop for one entire year. So, I called it a "vacation" even though it was a forced vacation. I was smiling on the outside, but crying inside.

Commencement: June 2009 - 11 yrs. Old - A.A. Degree Summa Cum Laude.

My year waiting for a scholarship was not completely lost. I always wanted to be inside of the oceans to see the beautiful deep water life. My great happiness was that I realized my dream. It made my "vacation" very sweet. A lady from Arizona, who doesn't want to be named, gave me a scuba diving scholarship. I got my certification as open ocean water scuba diver, and I went for many dives. I could see and touch the ocean floor. I could examine the extraordinary creatures and things seeing only in books. I shared the deepness of the ocean with stingrays, colorful fishes, and exotic creatures. I was a few feet away from a school of dolphins and I was able to touch them. These were great moments of my life. In the soundless world of deep water, without any doubts, I perceived the echoes of the Creator's Presence.

Pool Training   Finally, I am a Certified Scuba Diver   First Dive

My faith in the Creator led me to believe somehow that I would find a solution to my problem. Ultimately, I found some comfort. In 2010, I decided to apply to many universities. I took much into consideration before I decided where to apply for my last two years to get the bachelors' degree. I prayed for scholarships. The results of my prayers and labor went beyond my wildest expectations. I applied to seven universities; five accepted me and four offered scholarships. I could not believe that in the space of one year in which I stopped made such big difference.

Scuba diving deep in the Ocean, Anacapa, CA.

Inside Skydiver, Las Vegas NV

My first choices of schools were The University of California Los Angeles and Stanford. UCLA offered me the full Regents' Scholarship. I could not be happier. This scholarship scared me a lot. I would need to perform above my abilities. I became a Bruin Regent's Scholar. It worried me. I borrowed my father's shoes to walk in (his spirit and strength) and my mother's Confucius mind (her tranquility and patience). I felt well rewarded for my resilience and hard work.

I believe that if anybody tries hard, sometimes very hard, will succeed as well or better than I did. Is true, we will have our moments of despair and panic but we need persevere. On my first four quarters at UCLA, I received all good grades except 3 B+'s. This proves beyond a doubt that I am not a genius like some people say and that I am not perfect.

CHAPTER 4:

FACING OBSTACLES
AND OVERCOMING DISILLUSIONMENT

My life's disappointments are just a few. When I experience events going against me, I think two ways: At a certain point, the bad events will end and I need to be resilient and patient and wait until the good waves start to come ashore. The sun always will rise over the darkness. When the right time comes, it will happen. Second, we need to understand life and the "natural events" that occur. For example, many base individuals do terrible acts for personal gains. This is the nature of the human beast. To understand this process and let go and not revenge for acts done by base persons is divine.

In a Daily News report by Dana Bartholomew about higher education [Los Angeles], a study by Nancy Shulock, executive director of the Institute for Higher Education Leadership and Policy at Cal State Sacramento stated: "[Our] study shows that LA Community Colleges lag behind others across California, with only one in four students fulfilling their goal of earning a certificate or associate degree or transferring to a four-year university… We've got to reverse the trend…The problem is that not enough students are finishing the academic program ... not enough students who begin are finishing." [5] Also in the same article, it states that: "Critics of the LACCD say that its performance not only puts thousands of student dropouts at risk of lower-paying livelihoods, but fails to prepare a statewide workforce that will need 1 million new college grads by 2025".[5]

In my opinion, East Los Angeles College, a college of 27,000 students, and its ASU (Association of Students) were dead (and continue to be) or at least critically dormant needing emergency care. They accumulate a great amount of the money though parking fees and this amount seems to disappear in a black hole. Nothing was done to the benefit of the students besides the innocuous "Spring Flings (party)," Halloween parties, and food bashes to make money (?) for students' clubs. Everything was around food: barbecues, tacos, and the whole enchilada. I did not observe any scientist, politician, writer or any member of the thinking elite to be invited to our campus to light the student's heart, imagination, or understanding. At ELAC, only 20% of the students graduate and 8% transfer, which is a shameful number for any college.   The Professors are excellent and they are masters of what they do but they do not have the needed help from the administrators.

Because all that, I decided to run for ASU president. The ADSA (Associated Dean of Student Activities) did not look with good eyes on my plan. She said: "To be a president, you need to represent the college in the meetings with the board. You should run for another position". She showed me with no doubts that she would rule. I knew that I would lose but it was a question of principles.

In the day before starting the campaign, when ADSA was meeting with us about the rules of the campaign, I could see without doubts her partiality and favoritism for my opponent. I thought that when you are in a college you are there to learn. ASU presidency should to be for the benefit of all students and not for benefit of the administration, and to act pretty in front of the board. I decided to run. My principles forced me. I declined her advice and it became an all out war. I made clear that I would be my own man and would run for the presidency. I recognize that I would not win because she was the elections powerful judge and czar. It looked like Stalin's Russia. She enforced the rules, and policed the behavior of the candidates. She was in charge of counting the votes and most important she was the one who kept in her office the urns with the votes overnight. I knew that she would act with partiality in favor of her handpicked and favorite candidate.

The ASU elections are rigged from the beginning in the way it is organized. Only one candidate was chosen to run for each position and unopposed and I broke the balance (I forced her approval). I took pictures of her favorite candidate breaking the rules and many other actions that would impeach completely my opponent's candidacy. One of the rules was about the places not allowed for posting the campaign ads. Next day, I saw her favorite candidate's ads to be all over the campus and about eighty percent in illegal places. I went to talk to the ADSA and she said she would take care of it. Two days passed and nothing. Later, I saw them together, the ADSA and her favorite candidate, putting ads side by side, for both the "Spring Fling" party and for her candidate using the Students Activities vehicle (a school owned golf cart).

I had enough pictures to prove this overwhelming partiality in favor of my opponent including my opponent asking for votes a few feet from the voting booth. I took them to the Vice President of Student Services and he became very upset at me because I brought this to his attention. He closed his eyes and let things go by. He decided that was better to close his mouth and not to act. The ADSA and the VPSS were making a mockery of the students' wishes and of the democratic process.

This mockery keeps on. One year later, in the 2010 elections, another candidate (at least they had two candidates), the one that was not liked by the ADSA was disqualified because allegedly he was asking for votes a few feet from the voting booth. The same act that my opponent did (I still have the pictures). This time the ADSA inverted the ruling! It is very interesting.

The ADSA succeeded in derailing my campaign, but the school and the education in general suffered a huge defeat. I did not become mad because this is the nature of the beast. I knew that my chances were very small to win because I had only a few bucks to run for election ($35 dollars to be exact), and my father put many restrictions on my campaign because of my age.

I sent an e-mail to V.P. of Student Services and to the college president. The VPSS ignored my e-mail with the pictures of the irregularities. He was in charge of the Scholarships and he black listed me. I applied for scholarships based for merit and need. They had $175,000 to give in scholarships and I got zero. No student of the class of '09 got better grades than I. In the graduation booklet, my name was not mentioned that I graduated with honors. They cut my Meza resources. Merits at ELAC mean nothing. Brown nosing and being subservient is what counts.

I believe that it is better to lose with integrity than to win with dishonesty. It was a learning process. What I learned in this election was that many "educators" teach that it is OK to cheat to win. I disagree. I deem as truth that what one dishes out will come around, here or there to bite them back.

One that does good deeds and is honest will win when the right time comes. Maybe one loses some battles but not the war. If you are honest and work hard many doors will open for you and the ones that close are the ones you should not go in.

The ELAC administrators negated my honors but it was offset and blown off by the Certificates of Recognition from The United States Congress, The California Senate Education Committee and the City of Monterey Park and a Letter of Recognition by the California Governor Arnold Schwarzenegger. I proudly hang them on my bedroom walls.

At that time, I was running kind of nervous because I did not have any scholarship. A miracle happened, the UCLA doors opened for me. They gave me the most prominent Scholarship, the Regent's Scholarship. My academic future is assured. Now, I am scared to be a thirteen years old senior (last year to graduate) in a great university but trusting in the Almighty's blessings and in my work. If I don't deviate to pursue any other concurrent endeavor, I will graduate in 2012. I am very attracted to learn to fly airplanes and get a scuba diver instructor certification and other endeavors. If I pursue them maybe I graduate one year later, but I am not after records, I am after my betterment. I shall persevere. **Remember: When your time comes, it will happen**.

MY VIEW OF LIFE

This was a hard section for me to write. I do not like to share my inner thoughts because they are the essence of my being. It is like me disrobing my soul in front of others. I do not like to be in the limelight. I like to do my own thing and be left alone. I only expose my inner feelings with hope that I may lead some kids to see my success and believe that they can do the same or better. If one kid can accomplish it or go far beyond because my book, I will be overjoyed.

Now, when I compete, I do not compete with others for whatever reasons it may present itself to me. I do not measure myself by comparing with others' records. I march at my own beat and when I compete (for example martial arts), I compete against my own self. The trophies are collateral gains. If somebody else gets the gold, I do not mind. If I do not show improvement, I feel like a loser even though I got gold. Many people told me to accelerate my studies to be the second youngest student in the U.S. ever to get a bachelor degree. Au contraire, when I was forced to stop one year for lack of money, I made lemonade out of this lemon. I took some classes to help my development, I took time to write this book and I went scuba diving and got my certification.

We should not try to be like anybody else. If we are like anybody else, we are not ourselves anymore and we lose our innate ways to be. Our precious being became a mere imitation of others. It becomes a false gold, a fool's gold. We should be the best that we can be. Improving oneself is the key. I try to make at least one definite move daily toward my goal. Bruce Lee said in his book, "Tao of Jeet Kune Do": "Running water never grows stale. So you just have to 'keep on flowing.'"

If I see one person that has good qualities, this makes me happy and gives me hopes for a better society. More than that, I jump to the opportunity of getting important lessons by their actions or teachings to improve myself.

Second, I have my code of conduct. I do my best to respect all beings, to be just and to be truthful. Looking the immeasurable cosmos and the infinitesimal number of creatures under a microscope and their interactions I can see the Almighty.

The incredible genius of Einstein describes in a poignant quote my exact thoughts by stating:

"We are in the position of a little child entering a huge library filled with books in many languages. The child knows someone must have written those books. It does not know how. It does not understand the languages in which they are written. The child dimly suspects a mysterious order in the arrangement of the books but doesn't know what it is. That, it seems to me, is the attitude of even the most intelligent human being toward the Almighty. We see the universe marvelously arranged and obeying certain laws but only dimly understand these laws. Our limited minds grasp the mysterious force that moves the constellations" (Mike Jammer: Einstein and Religion).

People are free to interact with each other. If I find base and vile creatures in my path, I try my best to stay far away from them. I try to be myself and lets other be as they want. I am not a judge, far from me. This position belongs just to the One. I do not discuss religion. I try to be the best as I can and lead by example. I do not try to convert anybody to my beliefs or type of life. Freedom of choices is one characteristic of the Universe but these choices will reward or destroy one.

Many times I do not like what I see. The press and especially the liberal western TV desensitize people and make them believe that we are at a premium if we misbehave. They create horrendous reality programs showing people at their lowest and pay them to act as vulgar being. People believe that what they see is the way to be. The bad apples are spoiling their surroundings. It makes me sad but I remember that bad apples also are part of the creation.

I am very choosy about what I read and watch. I think that I owe it to myself to be the best I can and stay away from the vile behavior. I deem as truth that what you dish out will come around to bite you back, here, there or at anywhere at any time. People's behavior is diverse as the number of the people in the world. I do not become mad or offended when somebody acts badly towards me. We need to understand the nature of the beast.

Let's suppose that somebody is drunk or is a bully and wants to show off to others and call me a derogatory name. I understand this human attitude. What is my reaction? - I don't get offended at all and I just walk away smiling. If I let myself to become offended, I would feel upset or mad. These inside emotions sulk and darken the soul and it is not good for a healthy body. If I decided to fight, it would be worst. Somebody would be hurt or both could end up in jail. What is to gain? - **NOTHING.**

In turn, I walk away smiling because I walk away happy for not fighting and not having ill feelings toward anyone. By walking away, I do not give the bully the opportunity to show off. By walking away, I walk tall, intact, and with a good feeling inside because I performed well. I quote Bruce Lee: "The best fight is the one you don't fight". Let him eat his inside out because our lack of attention to his rhetoric.

What is the best way for us to win over this situation? - Work hard to succeed on our endeavors and don't look back. The bully will either understand that our approach is correct and mend his ways or it will drive him insane with hate by seen us basking under the sun of our success.

When I look at life, I see that we are mere sojourners in this earth. As visitors, the stopover is very short. I quote my father: "In a blink of eye, you find out you are old." We need to positively mark our stay in this world and do the maximum of our capacity to better this planet. We need act fast or it will be too late. Our biggest adversary is selfishness that imperils us to see the injustice of our actions and the crooked path that we may follow. Our heart sometimes refuses to grasp that only the good deeds, knowledge and wisdom can help us and our world.

"The ideals which have lighted my way and time after time have given me new courage to face life cheerfully, have been Kindness, Beauty and Truth." Albert Einstein

CODE OF CONDUCT

On my journey through this world, my code of conduct gives me a compass to abide by through all my life. From my father's teachings, I created my code as follows:

1) Be Respectful To All Creation.

No person is minimized by the words of a foolish one. I prefer to run than fight. My father tells me: "If somebody wants to fight, you should run at least three miles: the first mile in order not to hurt anyone, the second mile in order not to get hurt and the third mile in honor of your sifu that taught you to fight". I will fight only if I am against the wall and no way to escape or to defend someone in a great peril. This rule includes giving respect to all creation: animals, plants and the inert nature on this earth.

2) Be Truthful

I learn to tell the truth thanks to my parents. If I do something wrong, maybe my father will discipline or scream at me. If I lie, I will face severe punishment. I learn that facing the truth always makes me feel good inside. We make many mistakes in our lives. Facing and learning from our mistakes will make us stronger.

3) Be Just

If there is a situation in which somebody may suffer from any ill action from my part I must stop in my tracks and it is out of the question.

One day a cashier gave me a one hundred dollar bill in place of a ten dollars bill. I was in a hurry; I did not pay attention and I went home. Upon my arrival, I found out that a big mistake happened. I was astonished by how somebody was capable of a blunder like that. I was tired and I had my pocket full of money that was not mine. I needed to act rapidly. I got my father to give me a ride back to the store. When we arrived to the store at the exact time the cashier was recounting and recounting her money. She was nervous because her register was short. The old lady cried and gave me a hug and a kiss when I gave back her money. I knew that $90 difference would represent more than eight working hours of pay for her. That day was and still is precious to me. I won twice. My father, as a reward, gave me my first one hundred dollar bill ever for my act. When I remember this episode and it comes to the eyes of my mind, my heart rejoices.

4) Have Great Respect to Parents

We owe our life to them. They suffer, love, protect us, and they dedicate uncountable hours of their lives to us. We can do no less than to have the most regard for them. We need show that we appreciate their love. When they pass away, our hearts will be very sad but at the same time we will be happy because they experienced our love during their lives. Their smiles and happiness will be engraved on our soul, and it will have a soothing effect over our pain.

5) Do Not Move Away From Your Traced Path

During my campaign for Student President, my opponent did many things that were forbidden. A friend said, "Let's do the same thing." I told her that is better to lose with dignity than win with dishonesty. The wrong things that you put out are those that come back to you threefold.

6) Yong Wang Zhi Qian

Be Ambitious and March Forward Courageously, meaning We Can Do. Set your goals high and put your heart and brains in it. There is a quote that my father repeats many times from Governor Leonel Brizola, a Brazilian politician: "Eat the hot soup by the borders". The hot soup, in a large plate, seems impossible to eat without burning our tongue. But if one eats the soup slowly and methodically by the colder edges, one finishes it rapidly. Even a small move counts and everything starts with the first move. Chairman Mao Zedong said: "A march always starts with the first step". We need to give this first step with a full heart.

Bruce Lee's said: "One should transform oneself to the shape of the vessel". By conforming to vessels shape we will be liquid and not brittle. Liquids do not break and reach their destination easily. The key for our advance is to set goals, make the plans and focus on marching forward courageously and methodically every day. Be resilient and we should transform ourselves to the right shape depending of the needed response to the situation.

7) Education and Hard Work Matters

I know that if I work hard today when I am young it will mean a much better life decades from now. I know that knowledge will be my big brother walking with me during all my life helping me out when I am blue and low and sustaining me when I am in trouble. The wisest man ever, King Solomon, said: "Knowledge is more precious than gold and silver". Knowledge cannot be robbed or lost. I spent about eight hours studying six days a week and when I feel like not studying or when I am down, I remember what Muhammad Ali said: "I hated every minute of training, but I said, 'Don't quit. Suffer now and live the rest of my life as a champion.'"

CHAPTER 5:

STUDY METHOD

Some people consider me a genius, but I know that I am not. My accomplishments are due to thoughtful planning, strict commitment and discipline, and parental dedication. In the beginning, my parents did not have a clue on how they would educate me and their idea was to put me in a public school and that would suffice. With my first word spoken at a very early stage in my life and the recognition that this was a product of an interaction between the environment and me, everything changed.

From the beginning, my father had a gut feeling that it was important for me to have a strong audio/visual interaction to stimulate my brain lobes to develop and accelerate learning. This is the reason that he embellished my crib with lights, color, movements and shooting sounds. After my first words, he tried to enhance these interactions by working intensively procuring my response to objects that surrounded me. He tagged a name for each object that interacted with me. After awhile I knew the names of the familiar objects in my life and I would call for them. Since the early stages in my childhood, I would call out 'botte' when I wanted milk. Also when I saw a bottle, I excitedly responded by babbling the word 'botte'. Every time we went out, my father spent most of his time showing me things and tagging a name for each thing on my vision span and doing his best for me to see the interrelation between them. It was a hard job.

Every day after work and in any of their free time, my parents spent many hours interacting with visual/audio stimulus and me. They put aside a determined number of hours to work with me. When the cards were introduced with the objects that surrounded me, the speed of learning advanced twofold. The important point was that my parents never gave up in this continuous work. Sometimes they were discouraged because the fruit of their work was not evident, but they were resilient.

Shortly after mastering single words came the two word process like see tiger, hide tiger, pronounce, make sound … (The action for see tiger, hide tiger would be turning the card with the picture for me to see and turning the card to its other side containing the word tiger and pronouncing 'tiger' and make its sounds). Teaching math would be the same system. Show one toy car and say one car, adding another car and say two cars and vice versa.

The next step became more structured by setting up strict hours for learning and rest. Making classes mix with toys and play made me welcome this learning interplay. My mother tells me that each time she finished a class, I would cry. Because of my response, she was encouraged to make the tutoring longer. My parents usually taught me four to five groups of half-hour instruction/interaction and later added more and more time. The days that I was sick or not cooperative they would work fewer hours with me and include more breaks. The break time was dependent of the day and circumstances usually varying from ten minutes to half hour. However, she would try to work with me every possible time. When my mother quit her job, my parents started instructing me in seven forty- to fifty-minute classes per day.

As soon as I graduated from the two words program my mother introduced the complete single sentences like: Mama opens eye, Moshe opens eyes. All of these sentences were accompanied for some kind of action. She also started using very easy books. Math continued in direction of a more complex addition and subtraction.

After that, I evolved to books used by schools and those that my parents thought to be good placing emphasis on English, Math and Sciences. The first books were kindergarten books and they were very easy and we covered them quickly. My parents bought books that followed up the ladder (that is: first grade, second grade and so forth). The books used by the public schools seemed so silly easy that I wandered why the students took so long to cover them? When I became seven years old, I already had covered all (and more) the twelfth grade high school math books and about the seven grade English.

My parents' technique on Math: They would choose four to seven problems already solved in the book and go over with me or they would solve a few problems showing step by step and later they would give the same problems for me to solve by myself from the beginning. I would try to solve them and I would explain to my parents how I went about to solve them. If I had a mistake or if I had a road block, they would show me again and repeating the same steps for the solution of the problem as much as I needed to grasp the though process. **Extreme patience was the key**. For example, they went over seven problems with me and when it was my turn, I solved five of them by myself and if I had one wrong and one that I couldn't solve, they would go over all the solutions covering all the problems, including the two challenging ones. Subsequently, they would give me a new group of five problems plus the two ones that I had difficulty with. This method was repeated over and over until I mastered all problems presented.

When I was eight years old, my English was up to the ninth grade. I was slower in English and it has always given me trouble. When you know more than one language, it is hard to master one of them. I became a jack of all trades but a king of none.

My parent's technique for English: The study of single and simple sentences stressing the grammar and vocabulary. This was the core in learning English. Instead of reading literature books, my parents would choose books about science, inventions and how to do or make things. Later, they would let me choose books about topics that would appeal to me but with their guidance. The books that usually would allure my imagination were about people and epic happenings that changed the world, astronomy, martial arts, extraordinary thinkers and other things alike. Most of the books considered literary classics that were used in schools did not appeal to me.

I love to read books about sciences, inventions and how things come about. Most of my scientific knowledge came from books that I went over with my parents. Actually, I did not follow the high school curriculum in some subjects. My parents would focus on the subjects that they felt more important for my education. Some subjects studied in high school were ignored completely. I am very weak, for example, in Biology and all-purpose Music. I did not like Biology since I have an aversion for dissection and dead animals. I declined to take Biology in college because the curriculum asked the students to dissect a cat. As an amateur pianist, music for me is overkill. I play the piano reasonably well, and I do not want be a professional musician. Why should I learn the number of strings that a cello has or what an oboe is? It makes no sense to me. A class that I was forced to take in College was Music Appreciation. It is OK for those that do not know to play any instrument. I know how to play the piano and I do not want to be a professional musician and this is enough in my books.

At seven, after I was denied to take an entrance test at LACC, my parents started to prepare me for tests. They knew that I would face this situation in the future. They acquired test books like SAT, English, and Math and I put aside one hour daily to practice the tests.

Finally, when I was eight years old, I had the opportunity to take an entrance test. I passed and I was accepted in college. The first year of college was not challenging at all because I took the same subjects that I already knew well. I took Intermediate/ Advance Algebra (I was in Calculus level and those Algebras corresponded to twelve grade high school and first-year College) and Martial Arts (Wushu – Staff). I wanted to take Calculus, but my father thought that it was too much for me to deal with. He wanted straight A's to assure that I would get a scholarship in a great university. He believed that if I would take classes on my level probably I would get a mix of B's and A's but not good enough to get a full scholarship with a full tuition and expenses paid. He exchanged speed of graduation for certainty of scholarship. He was right and I gained much following his lead.

The second tactic was to use "prep time," i.e., my free time that I had between classes and easy subjects to prepare always for what was coming ahead in the next semester. It consisted of buying the subject books for the classes that I would take next semester and going over it a few months before the actual classes.

All the time that I was in college and up to now, the tactics are the same: master the subjects for the next quarter. Planning is essential. I go talk to the professor about the books that he uses and if the classes that are slated to happen next semester/quarter will really happen as scheduled. During the classes, a tactic that I consider very important is to establish presence in the classroom and to take control of the environment by imposing the awareness of my presence to all classmates and professors: I sit in the front, I ask and answer all possible questions and if I err, I am still learning. I pay maximum attention in class, I always try to turn in the homework ahead of the time, solving extra questions (i.e.: solving more problems than the ones asked), go to the professor in his office and ask important questions in the future chapters to be covered (it usually impresses them) and I am always cordial with everybody (this is my nature) and tutor or help my classmates (it helps me to get stronger in the subject). Bringing students to my level of understanding is always a pleasure and a good way to make friends.

I applied to different universities and I was accepted by the majority of them (two didn't accept me) but UCLA; a top school in the U.S. and in the world, not only accepted me but gave me a full Regent's Scholarship and other scholarships that covers all my tuition and my expenses (Compare with ELAC!!!). The strategy in this great global effort came with real gold.

I am still using the same strategy at UCLA. My first year at University, I got all good grades except 3 B+'s (which proves that I am not a genius). My first B's ever were probably due that UCLA uses a quarter schemes (a faster pace than a semester), not being used to the UCLA class system, much greater standard than my previous college and that I am dedicating more time to extra-curricular activities. This is not an excuse. It is an assessment. Excuses are not good for anything. Assessment is important to analyze, change course of action or correct mistakes if needed.

To maintain the Regent's scholarship, it requires a B average and I am using it well for my advantage. The first quarter was time consuming and quite challenging because everything was new but now, I am applying this time not necessarily for a grade A, but to accomplish other goals. So, instead of all A+s, I am exchanging them for accomplishing more sought endeavors. I know that the expectative of being a perfect human being is flawed but the expectative to do the best as one can is attainable. So, I will have a few more B's in the future. I can live with that.

STUDY MODE

Study mode, for me, is the production of maximum learning in a minimum time. I need to procure the ideal situation to produce the study mode. I need to have slept a minimum of eight hours and the best would be to study after a nine hour sleep. I cannot study in a bed or in a sofa because it drives me to sleep. Studying in a park, in a library, or in a place where there is too much traffic, I get distracted and I start to look around observing my surroundings. UCLA has a room in the library where I can close the door and isolate myself from distractions. My home is the best place to study. The best scenario for a good learning production is to have a chair and a table large enough to put my books, laptop, notebooks, pen, and whatever junk I need. If the seat of the chair is uncomfortable, I lose concentration and I do not stay there for long. The seat and the table need to be proportional to each other. A tall chair that forces the back to bend while typing or working, it is bad for the back and health. My father bought me a comfortable and cushioned chair. Sometimes, I forget that I am sitting. In conclusion, I need to be well rested in a place with no distractions with a comfortable seat being proportional to a table where I can put all my stuff.

Once I know my classes' hours, I make a plan. For each one hour of class, I study a minimum the double of hours and divide in two halves: One to go over the material before being presented and the other to go over the material covered in class. If I do not understand something, I put more time on it, and I make sure to go over with the teacher in the next class or during his office hours. This is essential. Remember I am not a genius and I kept my grades well above average because this technique. I make sure that my free time is to study the subjects that I consider I know enough to get a B but not an A and to study for the next term classes.

On average, I study two sections of two to two and a half hours (daily) and I force myself to have a break of 15/30 minutes. During the break, I walk around, get a snack, sit by the window, or do whatever and I return to study according to what is planned for that day. I do not study all day long. I plan two to four hours of free time every other day and I do a variety of things that I like, for example, exercise, practice martial arts or piano, read or study things that I love like airplanes, oceans, universe, etc. Now, I am trying to master ice skating. If I have to study for a test or exam, or I need to turn in a paper or I feel insecure, I do not have any problem to occupy my free time hours. School comes first. If I need, I will occupy all my free week hours and laziness is not part of my routine.

During the weekend, I will stay away from my studies unless I feel that I didn't master the subjects covered on prior classes. I spend around sixteen hours during the weekend for my pleasure: It starts in the dinner on Fridays and ends at lunch on Sundays - I do not study or think about what I will do during my "free time". I just go with the flow. I go out with my parents, eat out, rest, sleep as much as I want, watch TV (if there is something good – usually not), read, play soccer, etc. and do whatever comes up on my head. My tactics when I am forced to study a subject that I don't like is to mix what I like to study and what I don't like to study (maybe changing subjects every hour) or to have smaller breaks in between. But no matter what, I will study what I have to study. **Resilience is the key**. Need to conquer or be conquered. The period of the time one forces himself to study is tough, but when one is finished with this agony, one feels like a winner. Now, when I look behind all my hard times endured, I feel like a champion.

CHAPTER 6:

MY PARENTS AND I

I believe that in the first seven years the parents should guide with discipline and love and after that, let the children be free in small incremental steps. Let them to know if they act well, and they will be rewarded with more love and freedom. This is what my father tells me.

My mother is my pride and joy. I encounter all the love that I need on her. She quit her job to dedicate all her time to me to which I am grateful. Since I went to college at eight years old, she sits in the front of my classroom, whether it is winter or summer, cold or hot, rain or shine, to protect and take care of me. She walks, drives, jokes and plays with me. She is my confidante and companion 24/7. My mother never punishes me and we have our secrets. If I misbehave, she tells me that she will notify my father. Many times she does not tell my father about my misbehavior, but when she tells I know that I am in trouble because my father is straight as an arrow. What it is, it is. No excuses. One misbehaves, one is punished. It is like that story of good cop, bad cop.

My mom is my confident and companion 24/7.

My father's goal is to make me more independent. I am too young and most of the things I do depend on his authorization. When I am with him, I have no worries. He leads me. Now, he lets me make more decisions but I know that he still ogles like a hawk to all my movements. In the beginning, my father used to plan my daily activities. Now, he advises and I plan. Every week, we have a family sitting in. I tell him my schedule, my parents make suggestion or changes, I redefine and my father approves. I take from there. I do my best not to deviate one step away from the planning. Every week is planned carefully, and it is essential that I follow through to successfully accomplish that step. My father is kind of ill and I hope that he endures many years to be at my side guiding me.

It is important to learn that we need to mix the good with the bad and take them as they come. We need to understand when we master a subject fast and well we will be rewarded. For example, scuba diving was a great challenge to me. I was being trained to take out the mask, clean it, and put it back as exercise at fifteen feet under water. This was very difficult because the water invades the nostril and it is difficult to take a breath. It is essential not to panic. My father used to scuba dive in the army, and I did not know how he found out about my difficulties since he stayed at home during all my classes. My father telephoned my instructor: "Compel Moshe to do this exercise over and over again until he will do it not only correctly, extremely well and precise. If not, he will not dive in the ocean". **Practice, practice and more practice are the keys for success.**

During my boat dives, my father was kind of sick and stayed on the boat. He told me that he was only a little worried because he trusted that I was well trained. He wanted to scuba dive with me in the deepness of the ocean but I needed to learn to act independently in stressful conditions. Now, I mastered the scuba maze. My reward is to share the deepness of this exotic habitat with beautiful oceanic creatures.

My father always accompanies me the first time in any adventure that he considers risky. I feel very secure with him. He is a rock. He can face anything. After my first experience with him, all feels well. I remember when I was eight years old and very scared to take a ride in a hot balloon. Flying high inside a hot basket was not a thrill for me. My father took me anyway against my will and during all the flight he held my hand. He took me to pet a lion cub in Las Vegas. The first time is always scary, but conquering the fear is great. He teaches me not to fear by example. He faces his health impediments with chutzpa and this teaches me to be strong and resilient. An important point in the relationship among us is that every night before bedtime we do the family hug. This reminds us that we are a loving family and to imprint our great mutual love in our hearts.

My father is my hero.

CHAPTER 7:

RULES, REWARDS and PUNISHMENT

As far back as I remember, my father always warned me what might happen if I did not listen to him or if I broke a rule. Everyone in the house knows what the rules are because they are clear and very well articulated. This is an essential part in having rules. They must be followed with no deviance. I know that if I break any of the rules it will bring consequences. This is a very simple equation.

THE RULES:

1) Be truthful. What it is, it is. Lying brings doubled or threefold punishment promptly.

2) Never scream back or disrespect any older person, especially parents.

3) Never cuss or use expletive language.

4) I must do the best I can in whatever I do. If not, do not even start it.

5) If I am misbehaving, I get a warning to stop. After the third warning, I will be well punished.

6) If I break a promise, I will be punished. My word must be unswerving and dependable.

7) If I screw up very big in something, I will be disciplined.

It has been over two years now that I have not been punished, which is a relief for me.

REWARDS:

My family does not celebrate my father's birthday (only mother's and mine), commercial and commemorative days like Father's Day, Mother's Day or other types. My father believes that if someone loves somebody it should be celebrated everyday with respect and love from one to another. Therefore, sometimes out of the blue, he bring us gifts, takes us out to eat, to the park, to museums, or some other place.

I am not rewarded for those accomplishments that come easy, for example, doing well in a sport that I enjoy like soccer or scuba diving. The practice of these sports is itself a reward. Some other actions are not pleasant and we need to work hard to accomplish. To study a subject that is unattractive or challenging shows effort. It is important for us to learn that we need to mix the good with the bad and take them as they come because this is life. When I bring my father some news that he considers as a great advance for my future such as an A as a final grade or other enterprise that he sees that I did my best he usually says: "Today is Father's Day. Let's commemorate". This commemoration usually ends up by him doing something that I like very much. Other times he asks me what I would like to have or to do. If I get an A, he praises my performance, but it is certainly not a "Father's Day."

In my house, we only celebrate some days in December when gifts are bought and given. My birthday gifts are usually a trip or something special that I ask (I remember all my birthday gifts): At 6 yrs. old, I started to train Wushu in the park. In the other birthdays, I asked to: Participate in the International Martial Arts Competition in Pomona; Ride a Hot Balloon in Temecula; Ride a biplane in Oceano; Visit the Egyptian museum in San Jose; Participate the *Today* show in New York; Do some Indoor Sky Diving in Las Vegas; and Visit the Atomic Testing Museum in Las Vegas.

PUNISHMENT:

I was very afraid to write this section. An unqualified opinion can cause widespread suffering and I cannot deal with that. I asked my father to write it. He is the one in charge of the punishments in my family; therefore, he is more qualified to discuss its merits.

MY FATHER'S WORDS:

Disciplining young children is one of the key jobs of any parent but whether or not that discipline should include spanking or other forms of corporal punishment is by far a trickier issue. The American Academy of Pediatrics does not endorse spanking for any reason because they concluded that spanking is not effective as a long behavior-changing. Tulane University, after studying over 2,400 youngsters, found out that those that were spanked more frequently at age three were more likely to be aggressive by the age of five. Duke University researchers revealed that infants who were spanked at twelve months scored lower on cognitive tests at age of three.

There is no point in rules if there is no consequence for breaking them. Those consequences need to be both realistic and educational. Love and discipline are extremely necessary for a normal growth. Every child needs to feel loved and secure. Discipline without love is worthless. With no discipline, the child will be a brat growing up to be a juvenile delinquent or worse. So many times the best laid rules are ignored "just this one time" by a parent who can't bring himself to stick to them.

The rules must be well known without any question. The children must know what they did wrong, what was wrong with it, the alternative that they should have done and what the consequences are. The objective of discipline is that a youngster when he grows older to be in charge of himself and his environment. To reach this objective, it is important that all opportunities be available for the child to be compelled to take responsibility for his actions.

Taking responsibility for an infraction always requires that the child understands what he did wrong and what they should have done instead in order not to repeat the same infraction. The most important is the child to know that he did wrong and take responsibility for the infraction.

When I punish my son, I strictly follow these important steps:

1) Parents should never discipline a child when they are angry. Parents should never be abusive. This is not discipline. Disciplining when the parent is mad may lead to uncontrolled anger and the child can be hurt emotionally and physically with severity.

2) Never use expletive languages at the child, and never call him faulty names like stupid or other derogatory terms. Always make him understand that you love him and that he is intelligent. Explain that we all make mistakes and he is being punished by his behavior and not for his being. He is not stupid just because his behavior was stupid.

3) When parents discipline, the child they **should never yell** at him or her. Always talk calmly to the child, showing that they are in control.

4) Be right and clear in your mind of the facts. **Never blame him for wrong facts.** You will lose your credibility.

5) When you discipline, **talk with warmth in a loving way**, showing what he did wrong and how he should act and what are the expectations.

6) Both parents must act in unison. The parents should never disagree about the punishment, fight or argue in front of the kids.

7) The parents should make sure to show to the child that they do not want to discipline him but they are forced to do it because of his behavior. Every time that I discipline my son, I do my best to show him that I am hurt equally when I punish him.

8) The few times that I spanked my son, I used a Chinese shoe, Bruce Lee style, and I spanked him a maximum of five times in the gluteus maximum. **Never hit a child in any other part of the body, never hit with anything else that can harm him in anyway and never kick, slap or punch your child.** An adult hitting a child with his regular strength can cause extensive damage to the child's delicate body. I punish not to hurt but to scare.

9) When you tell the child that he will be punished **never backtrack**. You may punish him with lower level of punishment but your word is important.

The reason why I do not endorse spanking to treat child misbehavior it is because parents go overboard most of times doing more damage than help. I prefer punishing in other ways. Yes, I spanked my son and in the few times that I did it, I paid strict attention to my rules of spanking cited above very seriously. Today with the results of my son's upbringing and looking back, I would do it all over again.

I know that many parents were harshly treated as children. They are afraid that real discipline wounds their child or they feel guilty for something, usually a divorce, and they think that leniency equals love. The worst situation is that many parents are too involved with their own life and don't want to take the time and energy to raise their child. For me, it is too selfish for a parent not to take time to nurture and correct their offspring. Single parenting and step parenting is not the ideal situation but love will conquer.

CHAPTER 8:

BEING IN THE PUBLIC EYE

A local TV station heard that I entered college at the age of eight years old. They surprised me by being on the campus and asking me for an interview. My mother called my father and he said it would be OK. The interview was retransmitted to other local and national TVs, and newspapers. Somebody sent a video to YouTube and it exploded on the internet. Since then, many other TV interviews and programs that I participated in were placed on YouTube, on the internet and there are numerous websites carrying them.

To be in the public eye brings many undesirable comments, critiques, and misinformation. I do not pay attention to those that want to put me down but some comments are very puzzling indeed and they show the human nature as its best and worst. Being realistic, I expect that and some.

Some people outright criticize me, cuss me or make awful remarks without knowing me. I take this a great lesson to understand the human soul and behavior. I try to travel through their inner feelings of frustration, foolishness, jealousy, petty posture and lost bearings. All of that for me is no more than cries to the wind. I wish I could help them to change their wicked ways.

Do you take to heart on what a drunken or a foolish person says? I don't pay any attention and it does not make me mad or upset. If I would become mad at their foolishness, it would bring harm to my being and my inner harmony would cease. I take it as a passing wind that just strokes my hair and gives a way for a new happening. On my part, I do my best to follow the golden rule, and I keep my respect for all the Creation in this Universe.

When anybody accomplishes something good, it makes me happy. I have high hopes that more people can accomplish more for the good of this universe. Jealousy and envy will destroy a jealous person and the people around. The truth is that everybody is good in some endeavor and they will do better than others. Perfection is not attainable. Don't criticize but praise. Be happy when somebody does something good. The world needs more of it. World peace and harmony is what I yearn.

In a website, it was published that my parents divorced. Since my parents did not know about their "divorce", I went to my parents solemnly and gave them this grave notice. This was good for a few laughs but sad at the same time for the misinformation.

Another website stated that I have ADD (Attention Deficit Disorder) and I need to use "Ritalin" (the official medication for ADD) all my life. I do not use any kind of medication and I am blessed with a good physical and mental health. Yet another website went to extreme to show two pictures: One was mine and the other shows a kid (about five yrs. old?) writing on a blackboard. The kid is not me for a fact. I wonder why people go to enormous effort to misrepresent the truth. Sometimes, it is hard for me to understand human behavior

Different websites and comments affirm with absolute conviction that my father is Israeli, Italian, Brazilian, Iranian and Iraqi. They also state that I was born in New Jersey, Pennsylvania, and other places. The true is that my father was born in Brazil of Italian/ Portuguese/German/Polish ancestors. I was born in California. My website, www.moshekai.com has my real pictures and there I have answers to the many questions that I am constantly asked. Sometimes it is tiresome to try to correct the lies over and over again.

RELIGION

Religion, for me, is an individual choice. Justice should be the mentor. I believe in a Creator, All Powerful. This belief empowers me to go always one leap beyond with no fears. The Creator already showed me His Graciousness by showering me with more blessings than I can count. I am deeply gratified and thankful to the Almighty. Blessed be He.

"My religion consists of a humble admiration of the illimitable superior spirit who reveals himself in the slight details that we are able to perceive with our frail and feeble mind…" **Albert Einstein**

Without knowing me, people tell that I am Buddhist (maybe because my mother is Chinese or my martial arts instructors are Shaolin Monks), Jewish (because my name – but ask a learned Rabbi about my situation of a son of a non-Jewish mother), Christian (because of many of my comments about Christians) and Taoist (because I cite some Taoist quotes) and even they tell that I am Presbyterian!   As a mathematician, I know that all the above cannot be inclusive at the same time. There is only one truth.

The reason I do not mention my religion is that it is a private matter and it is nobody's business. It is a divisive matter that makes people to hate each other on the spot. I prefer to love all, including my critics. I can say that I am not atheist or agnostic because I have a firm belief in the Almighty that empowered me and showered me with many blessings. That is that.

I have friends of all religions. Believe or not, I have very good friends that are Buddhists, Jewish, Christians and Muslims. On my birthday party, all of them came and we had a friendly and good time together. I gathered different kind of foods in separate tables to each religion out of respect to all. I appreciate their friendship very much. It is an honor to have them as friends.

I wrote an essay on Religion during my school days for my English class and maybe this is a repetition of some of my thoughts and it goes like that:

"Religion is the opiate of the people" is one of the most frequently quoted statements of Karl Marx. I partially agree. I reason that a strong belief in some religion or deity brings strength and comfort to face death, sickness and misfortunes. On the other hand, many crimes and genocides are perpetrated in name of religion.

Looking at the immeasurable cosmos and the infinitesimal number of creatures under a microscope and their interaction, I cannot refuse the idea of a Creator. People are free to interact with each other. If I find base creatures in my path, I try my best to stay far away from them. I try to be myself and lets other be as they want. I am not a judge, far from me. This position belongs just to the One. I try to be the best as I can and lead by example. I do not try to convert anybody to my beliefs or type of life. Unbounded freedom of choice is one essential characteristic of the Universe.

Many times, I do not like what I see. The Western press and TV desensitize people and make them believe that one is at a premium if one misbehaves. They create horrendous reality programs showing people at its lowest behavior. People believe that what they see is the way to be. The bad apples are spoiling their surroundings. It makes me sad but I remember that bad apples also are part of the creation. This drives me to be very choosy on what I read and watch. I think that I own to myself to be the best

I stay away from the vile behavior. I deem as truth that what you dish out will come back around, here or there.

People's behavior is as diverse as the number of the people in the world. I do not become mad or offended when somebody acts badly towards me. I understand that is the nature of the beast. If you look at life, you see that we are mere sojourners in this earth. As visitors, the stopover is very short. My father says: "In a blink of eye, you find out you are old". We need to mark positively our stay in this world and do the maximum of our capacity to better this planet. We need to act fast or it will be too late.

Our biggest adversary is selfishness that imperils us to see the injustice of our actions and the crooked path that we may follow. Only the good deeds, knowledge and wisdom can protect us when the white snow invades our heads, our bones weaken and our eyes refuse to see. Religion, it is for me an individual choice. Justice and Goodness should be the mentors. I believe in a Creator, All Powerful. This belief empowers me to go always one leap beyond with no fears. The Creator already showed me His Graciousness by showering me with more blessings than I can count. I am deeply gratified and thankful. Bless be the Almighty

"I know this: The Almighty is not an accomplice to murder, and we cannot allow any religion to give The Almighty a bad name." **Sheriff Leroy David Baca, LA County Sheriff Dept.**

"UNHAPPY CHILDHOOD?"

A comment repeated many times was that I lost my childhood and my childhood happiness. It is certain that my childhood was different than the most kids. I can say this: I was and I am a happy fellow. Did I lose something? I think not.

I can only try to compare: True, I did not play in the park freely with other kids but I trained Martial Arts with other kids and adults in the park. This experience gave me training and stamina to shape my body and compete with top athletes; Yes, I did not play hide and seek with other kids. I played hide and seek in the ocean with fishes; meanwhile, I scuba dived inside of wonderful caves. I stroke and swim with friendly dolphins and I touched sea stars and urchins in the sea floor. It was an incredible sensation to be able to share this silent and wonderful world; True, I didn't play "Tag" with kids of my age. I played Monkey King and other characters in different plays with adults and kids; Yes, I didn't play "Marco Polo." I played the piano to rejoice my soul. I can keep on comparing much more but I think that is enough. Happiness in childhood for me is the loving care of parents and a good creative environment.

Unhappy?

I love to travel: New York - NY, Calico and Chico - CA.

I love Museums: Atomic Museum NV (with my friend Richard), Paradise & Fort McClellan - CA.

I love Adventures: Biplane. Helicopter and Cart rides.

Sad is the life of kids forced to work in inhuman conditions and who are sold and bought to a life in slavery. I wish the world would be more human.

When I meet with kids below my age, I feel like babysitting and in the position of a big brother. I do not like to play juvenile games or talk about elementary things but I force myself in order to bring some smiles on their faces. It is a very strenuous affair to me. Most of the time, soccer is the language that I talk and play with kids. My friends are generally older classmates or older martial artists. My best friend took class with me at my prior college and he is taking the same classes with me at UCLA. So, I prefer to interact with people on the same level of interest in sciences, math and sports.

Mankind, in my opinion, was created free to march under they own drums at their own speed and different steps in direction to the good or to the bad. Let's hope that there are more people marching in direction to the good. Let's not criticize those that are not like us and do not are not considered as a part of 'our group or our religion'. The Almighty created the elephants and the tigers, the cherry trees and the bushes, the good and the bad apples and all of them are necessary in this world. There is a need for diversity. We should not tell people what to do but lead with love and good actions. I follow the golden rule going after wisdom respecting all Creation. How and where a person decides to go brings its future consequences and rewards.

Answer to the Most Asked Questions

Many questions are asked (e-mail: kaihsiaohu@yahoo. com) and some of them puzzle me for its relevance or lack of logic. I do not answer questions about politics or religion and I do not engage in answers that just inflames the divisiveness. I carefully try my best not offend anybody because I am concerned with the feelings of other individuals. Sometimes, I fail.

I decided to answer the seventeen most asked questions whatever I think that they are frivolous or not and not in the order of most e-mailed. I will not answer those questions already explained in the book. I don't have enough time to answer all the questions e-mailed to me to which I apologize. I am 24/7 on the go.

Q1. How did you accomplish all of this still very young? -
I focus on my strengths:

- The firm belief in the Almighty that showered me with many blessings and gave me forces to go one step beyond;
- The love and caring of my parents;
- The search for knowledge. Only with knowledge we can acquire wisdom and wisdom is the vessel in we can help the creatures on this world and better the lives of our fellow human beings.
- The mind to plan and the strong will and resilience to follow it and a heart open for learning, failures and victories.

Q2. What are the sports that you like to practice the best? – I love Soccer and Scuba Diving. I like to practice Martial Arts to develop my body, mind and discipline.

Q3. What do you see in the future of the U.S. and the World? – What amazes me is the great number of times that this question was asked. I am young in the years and I am not clairvoyant. I am usually a very optimistic guy and I hope I am wrong in what I see. The U.S. is being destroyed by the liberalism, sexual deviance, promiscuity, and especially with the help of the news media, that is obliterating the young people's morality and civility. U.S. will sink like the great Roman Empire, if we maintain this mentality. U.S. needs to put education and civility first and restrain the liberalism that preaches no limitation for misbehavior.

The World will face very soon a huge conflict with great violence. On one side, we have the great liberal countries facing medieval ones. One is destroying the humanity by obliterating their moral fibers and the other destroying human lives by blowing themselves up and murdering innocent people with immense cruelty. There is not a sensible middle ground in which we can live and let it be. Extremism and hate will not take us anywhere. Like I said, I hope that I am wrong, very wrong.

Q4. Which places would you like to visit? - China, Taiwan, Brasil, Cuba, France, Vietnam, Thailand and Italy (not necessarily in this order).

Q5. Which politicians would like to meet? - Chairman Hu Jintao (China), Prime Minister Vladimir Vladimirovich Putin (Russia), Prime Minister Binyamin Netanyahu (Israel), Ex-President Lula (Brasil), and Fidel Castro (Cuba).

Q6. What is the best place that you visited? – The deepness of the ocean.

Q7. What are you more proud of? – This book. I have great hopes that I will be able to reach and help young people and parents.

Q8. What are your favorite personalities? - My parents, many of my professors, my martial arts sifus, Ming Lum and the distant ones Jet Li, Muhammad Ali, Tony Jaa, Einstein, Sun Tzu, Bruce Lee, Gandhi, Moses ... They are individuals from the past and present that I consider my Masters because I can learn from their lives and ideas.

Q9. What impacted your life the most? – The death of Popó Kuei. I still miss her very much.

Q10. What do you like to have that you never had? – A dog. Since I can remember, I have lived in apartments with no pet policies. I wish to feel really free by living in a house with many animals. I hope that someday we, my parents and I, will be able to live in a big house with many trees covered with fruits and flowers.

Q11. What would you like to have but you know that you are never going to have? – A yellow singing canary. I like to see and hear them, but I can't have this pleasure by imprisoning them in a cage. They deserve to be free.

Q12. What do you dislike the most? - Human suffering.

Q13. What is your IQ? - I know my IQ but I will not tell. IQ is just a number. I refuse to be represented by a number. I am not a digit and it is dehumanizing to me. Many so called high IQ people never did anything for the humanity. A human should be represented by his doings.

Q14. A website states that you drink alcohol and take medications. Is that true? I take medicine when I am sick. Even then, the only medicine that I remember taking was for a cold. However, the last two years I had flu shots early in the flu season and I did not catch any cold. One website claims that I have ADD (Attention Deficit Disorder) and I am forced to take Ritalin which it is not true. I am blessed with good health.

I have never tasted alcohol except wine. My family usually drinks a glass of wine with their meals. This is an Italian tradition. One glass is my maximum and only during the meals. The other kind of alcoholic drinks do not attract me at all. This does not mean that I never will drink an alcoholic beverage. Maybe I will someday but moderation will be the key.

Cigarettes are abhorrent to me. I do not smoke and I do not want or like to be in the same room with a smoker. If somebody smoking offers me a lift, I prefer to walk. Smoking does not make somebody chic or attractive. For me, it is the opposite.

I stay away from drugs. The day that one takes drugs, he puts his whole life in jeopardy. Once is one too many. I advise heartily to anyone never experiment with drugs no matter what are the circumstances.

Q15. What questions bothers you the most? – When a person asks me or affirms that I am a genius. I wish that people understands that with planning, work hard, being resilient and not deviating from the goals traced will succeed.

Q16. Do you play video games? - In one TV interview, I said that video games are bad for kids. I received many cussing e-mails and critiques. I didn't mean that all video games are bad. I used many for learning Math, Sciences and English and as I affirmed in another section that I enjoyed playing a video game called **Brainetics (www.brainetics.com)** which is great for math. Now, I am using a video game to learn how to fly. What I wished to say is that a majority of video games teach violence and sex. Parents should be attentive and filter those that are not good for the development of a child. The video that disgust me the most is a game that recreates the Columbine HS massacre with players assuming the roles of the gunmen to better their records. A California law against selling violent videos to minors was stroke down by the United States Supreme Court in an incredible recipe to dumb down the future of America. The kids are not protected against violence and the deterioration of American morals. It continues. What shame.

Q17. Do you have a girlfriend? – As a teenager, it is too early to think about a girlfriend or worse, a serious relationship. Schools are very liberal and do not teach kids to safeguard against themselves. Puppy love can easily expand to early explorations that can bring untimely suffering. The majority of the teenage mothers are forced to go in survival mode, compelled to work and out of school enduring hard sacrifices in the early life putting their future in peril.

The children are the collateral damage and their upbringings are jeopardized. We see a great number of kids with a single parent in the U.S. (The single parenthood is also caused by the high number of divorce cases - In California, more them fifty percent of couples are divorced and remarried a few times). My father told me not to hurry up to take the first bus appearing in the horizon. I should take my time to choose the right bus to take me all the way to my destination. There are many beautiful fishes in the ocean but some are poisonous. The right choice in this matter is fundamental for a well-built future. Now, I am on a mission to finish my studies with no time for digressions.

Photo by Sifu Yudeng

To succeed, one needs to work hard and put the whole heart on all endeavors.

CHAPTER 9:

THE FUTURE

At my age, my future is just muddy waters. Many doors are open. Which one I will choose is a paradigm. It will be what I decide and what the Almighty will permit. I know that I will keep on seeking knowledge. Only Wisdom will help our world to grow stronger and improve our humanity. I am not a Genius - far from me. I know and understand that the right recipe for progress is to acquire knowledge and wisdom through hard work and focused perseverance. This is my planned path.

I need to decide if I should graduate next year (2012) or stay a few months longer (early 2013) and accomplish other goals. Or maybe, I will stop for a year and have a vacation. I need to make many decisions.

My goals? - Learn to fly a plane, get a driver's license, go to some place in Asia for maybe a year to become a better Martial Artist (Shaolin Monastery to learn Kung Fu, or Beijing to learn Wushu or Thailand to learn Muay-Thai), learn another language, take some courses in physics, chemistry & engineering, and learn to ice skate.

Next step? - A master or a bachelor? - Theoretic physics, astrophysics, engineering or a dual with business.

Where? - UCLA, MIT, Stanford, Harvard, China's Tsinghua University, France's Sorbonne or a University that offers me a good scholarship. My preference will depend mostly on which university will offer me a scholarship.

The Prized UCLA Regent's Scholarship

THE UCLA AFFAIR

Now I am in the UCLA and I cannot tally my countless blessings. Many things in this university are different. What calls my attention is the professionalism of the UCLA Administrators compared with the ELAC Administration. The difference is remarkable. Here, it seems to me that they want students to learn and succeed in life. They care about academics, health and wellbeing. The resources are great. It is like a small city with all essentials. We have a full gym offering numerous machines and sports (including martial arts), we have a health clinic, a hospital, many restaurants and snacks places, many places to sit around and enjoy the surroundings, computer labs, different subject libraries, many workshops, many speakers, etc.

Somebody can get lost on the campus. UCLA makes it harder for students not to succeed. I feel happy and sad. I am very happy because of my scholarship, but I am sad that many students are struggling to pay for the high costs of a good education. Prices are sky rocketing. Many of the best students are being alienated. The lack of governmental funds pushes American Universities to accept more foreigner students in lieu of residents because they pay a higher tuition. The American politicians in general do not see that spending more money for education sustains the future of our nation. Putting education first is primordial for the survival of our country. More and more, we are importing foreign scientists or outsourcing our most important jobs and giving away our live hood, inventions and secrets.

My first day at UCLA as a Junior, September 23, 2010. Twelve Birthday.

CHAPTER 10:

HOW TO ENTER INTO A U.S. COLLEGE
AT AN EARLY AGE

In School:

During elementary and high school, one must study hard to get good grades, especially English and Math. After conquering these two subjects, one should go to the school principal and ask him to suggest classes that can be taken at a junior college or university. Most college and universities let high school and middle school students take classes during the summer break (if students have good grades). Choose a community college which is easier to enter and stay. If you do well, you can keep on taking classes there. Choose a class that you can do well in. Prepare yourself before. If you are not prepared or do not have time to study, you should not take any college classes because a bad grade will hurt you in the future.

In my case, my parents encouraged me to start college classes early with the backing of my home school counselor. If you show that you can handle your studies at school and can take charge of extra classes in college, it will be easier to get this recommendation from the principal. For two long years, I took classes at home and college simultaneously. Getting all A's helped me very much.

At Home:

At home, from the beginning, I worked hard on two important subjects: Math and English. Math always has been by far the one that I placed more hours and effort. Those two subjects are the basis for the entrance tests in any college and essential when taking SAT. I bought test books (for Math and English) including SAT test books and went over and over again solving the problems. I set aside at least one hour per day. I recommend any student to buy test books with solutions and go over them. Most of the students arrive at home and go play video, watch TV. They are not living their lives but observing other people's lives and letting their own lives pass by like wind in a summer day.

At College:

University can let you in especially during the summer but it is more difficult, formal, bureaucratic and expensive. Junior College is easier in the preceding four factors. My first try at Los Angeles City College the Dean of Academics did not even want to talk to me. He looked at the envelope but not at the content. You will find many of these not so bright bureaucrats. You cannot give up. You need to look around and try, try and try.

My second try was the golden try at East Los Angeles College. I was tested in English and Math. I did not feel prepared in English because my barely eight year old vocabulary was not very extensive. My surprise was that most of the high school graduates competing with me were not acquainted with the English idiom at all. This test situated me in an equal position with them. What a double shock: I was graded as average; meanwhile, many of the high school students flunked the exam. So, you should not be afraid. Mathematically, I was very strong going into the entrance test.

Take classes after school, take easy subjects or the ones that you know well at first to build confidence and make the professor believe in your ability. Taking a hard class in college and flunking will give you a bad record, stress, and lack of confidence all around. Maybe you will be forced to drop college before you really start. Be prepared. Only when one is prepared, can one take the college world.

CHAPTER 11:

PREDICTIONS AND SUGGESTIONS

The musts: We need to dominate at least a second language especially Chinese. Within the next 20 years, I believe that the Chinese language will dominate or at least be essential in the technical and financial markets. U.S. is slowing its scientific technologic speed due to a liberal agenda permeating in all sectors. The industry of sports and entertainment is dominating the American working market. They offer millions to the very small number that succeed in the sports and entertainment arena and they are on the everyday news sucking the imagination and influencing kids to follow them to be later faced with the harsh reality of failing and not making it.

Education is lagging behind each year and by the time this book is published the U.S. will not make the list of the top ten countries in sciences education. This attitude of not fostering education will have its consequences. At the same time, countries like China, Brasil and India are advancing at rapidly. The development of China schools and their sciences education will be well felt in the next decade. Taiwan and Israel are strong and advancing rapidly in technology due to need of education for their survival. We need change our backward displacement.

The education is "dumbing-down". "On history tests given to 31,000 pupils [by the National Assessment of Education Progress, the 'Nation's Report Card'], most fourth-graders could not identify a picture of Abraham Lincoln or a reason why he was important. Only 20% of fourth-graders attained even a 'proficient' score in the test. By eighth grade, only 17% were judged proficient. By twelfth grade, only 12% were proficient." [8]

When the NAEP history scores were reported, "The academic performance of New York state high school students in math and English. The results were stunning: Of state students who entered ninth grade in 2006, only 37% were ready for college by June 2010. In New York City, the figure was 21%, one in five, ready for college." [8]

According to a NFAP report "Only 12% of Americans are foreign-born. Even so, children of immigrants took 70 % of the finalist slots in the 2011 Intel Science Talent Search Competition, an original-research competition for high school seniors. Of the 40 finalists, 28 had parents born in other countries: 16 from China and 10 from India. In proportion to their presence in the U.S. population, one would expect only one child of an Chinese (or Indian) immigrant parent every two and a half years to be an Intel Science Search finalist, not as many in a year" [6]

Other musts: We need follow scientific careers to develop our knowledge of sciences. I see many of my classmates, not yet very knowledgeable in Mathematics been offered great jobs. The students in Engineering, Computer Sciences, Math, Physics and Bio Technology are well sought. If you did not notice, math is the basis for the most wanted technologies. Development of new technologies enriches any nation and makes it strong

Financially, the U.S. is in jeopardy but at this time its economy is pegged to China. U.S. made more paper dollars that it can pay by selling all the U.S. public and private sectors. China and Saudi Arabia have much of this IOU's in their power and both of them own many percent of the American industries and this is a critical problem. U.S. will have a nightmarish time if nations of the world will sell their reserve dollars and adopt another currency (like Iran and Venezuela are proposing). I am young and let's hope that I am wrong in my predictions but we need be prepared to any predicament that the future will bring us.

THE DONT'S

TV: When one is watching TV, he is observing his life pass by. He is not living his life but he is watching other people going about their lives. He is losing the opportunity to do something good to improve his life. I watch TV a maximum of three to four hours a week. The programs that I watch most are in the learning channels, so I see how things are made or when they go over a subject that interests me. I have two or three comedy programs that I like to watch. That's all. The problem that I see on American TV is that they glorify misbehavior, too much expletives, sex and violence. The news here is about Tiger Woods divorce; Lady Gaga Halloween dresses; Paris Hilton and Lindsay Lohan court cases; promiscuous Jersey shore crew drinking and fighting (and paid sumptuously for that!!!); etc... This is very disgusting. The reality TV shows in its majority is about people doing weird things or misbehaving. They do not have shows that are really important to improve the world with exception of the two learning channels. Taiwan TV start to imitate the American reality shows overlooking the Chinese respectful and beautiful ways of being and behaving.

VIDEO GAMES: Many young people spend a considerable amount of time playing video games killing their precious time on pastime tasks which will not help their future. The Asian Americans are by far the most videogame users in the U.S. In my opinion, the only thing that videogames can bring is maybe an artificial dexterity of the hands and eye movement. The top videogames sold in the US are how to steal a car and the black ops (war). Most of the top ten videogames are all about violence. Why not use videogames to pass the time, play and to learn at the same time? I used interactive videos that taught me Math, English, Geography, Sciences, Music, etc.

For example: **Brainetics (www.brainetics.com)** is a great instructional interactive video and play system. The multiple advantages with this system are: It teaches new math skills for all ages; provides kids free time to something constructive; give opportunity to parents to interact and participate some qualitative time with their children in a positive manner; and once they feel that math is fun and not a scary monster they start to use more math and enjoy their mathematical achievements.

Now I am using a software/video called Flight Simulator to get acquainted with flying an airplane. My goal is to master the art of piloting and hopefully somehow in a short future to start flying small airplanes and when the time comes to enter a real airplane I will be already ahead of the game.

INTERNET: Internet is extremely good for research but at the same time dangerous because the criminal minds floating in the web can allure young minds to extreme peril. In my opinion, YouTube, Facebook and Twitter are business and social tools. They are good for marketing, business, interaction and ego trips. They can do more damage than help for naïve users.

Chats with strangers in the Internet are for those lost souls that are falling in the empty spirals of their lives. They extend their hand to grasp something to help them not to fall but they only expose themselves to many dangers. I only use Internet Chat to converse with another student for information about classes and other subject of interest.

MUSIC: I recommend learning some kind of arts, especially learning some kind of musical instrument. I also consider writing and painting as very cool endeavors. Yoga, Tai Chi, Chi Gong, and meditation as very powerful mental and body exercises. When one is sad, down or bored, one may rejoice in those arts that soothe the soul and give strength to the body. I took classes on Yoga, Taiji and meditation.

I do not listen to rap or hip hop music. The English idiom employed in this type of music is not the correct one and the vocabulary is full of expletive words praising violence, sex and misbehavior. This is real disgusting. I prefer classic and easy listening where the words are like poems and the notes touch one's spirit. Frank Sinatra teaches English through his songs with a good vocabulary, perfect idiom and perfect pronunciation.

BOOKS:

Good books give guidance to daily existence and knowledge of the life. The books that I like to read at bed time are those that talk about people who made a positive difference. I also read about people and things that influence evils in our society like Hitler, Nazism, and others. I like books about sciences and especially books about the mysteries of the Universe.

My favorite books in my library:

Tao of Jeet Kune Do by Bruce Lee - Ohara Publications Incorporated – Santa Clarita California US – ISBN 0-89750-048-2

Mastery at Work by Nicole Grace – Mani Press – Santa Fe New Mexico US – ISBN 0-9747852-1-0

E=mc²: A Biography of the World's Most Famous Equation by David Bodanis - Walker and Company – NY New York US – ww.walkerboooks.com - ISBN 13:978-0-8027-1463-3

The Art of War by Sun Tzu translated by J.H. Huang. The Art of War: The New Translation. Quill William Morrow - ISBN 0-688-12400-3.

Einstein and Religion: Physics and Theology by Max Jammer – Princeton University Press - ISBN13: 978-0-691-10297-9

Marvelous Works of Zhen Ping Lu (**Calligraphy**) by USA International Chinese Talent Arts Association – LA USA - ISBN 978-9794457-7-4

APPENDIX 1: *TIGER CARD*

APPENDIX 2: *WE CAN DO - CHINESE EDITION*

Han Shian Culture
Publishing Corporation Ltd.

TEL: (02)2226-3070 #536
FAX: (02)2226-0198

3F, No. 150, Jian Kang Rd.,
Jhonghe City, Taipei Country 235,
Taiwan (R.O.C.)

http://www.101books.com.tw
E - mail: service@168books.com.tw

H30110 8歲進大學！地才少年凱孝虎的超強讀書方法

◎台灣母親的驕傲！新台灣之光。
◎震撼教育界的第一位台灣神童。
◆作者／凱孝虎
◆出版社／漢湘文化
◆出版日期／2011/06/02
◆21×28平裝書96頁

Novum Organum Publishing House Pte Ltd.
20.Old Toh Tuck Road, Singapore 597655.
TEL: 65-6462-6141 FAX:65-6469-4043

Novum Organum Publishing House(M)
Sdn. Bhd. No.8, Jalan 7/118B, Desa Tun Razak, 56000 Kuala Lumpur, Malaysia
TEL:603-9179-6333 FAX:603-9179-6060

BIBLIOGRAPHY

(1) Dekaban, A.S., Sadowsky, D., 1978. Changes in brain weight during the span of human life: relation of brain weights to body heights and body weights. Annals of Neurology 4, 345–356.

(2) http://pages.uoregon.edu/moursund/Math/brain_science.htm#   and Left Brain

(3) http://en.wikipedia.org/wiki/Broca%27s_ar

Broca's area in the left hemisphere and its homologue in the right hemisphere Broca's area is the section of the human brain (in the opercular and triangular sections of the inferior frontal gyrus of the frontal lobe of the cortex) that is involved in language processing, speech production, comprehension and computation. Math is a type of language. It can also be described as Brodmann's Area 44, and 45 and is connected to Wernicke's area by a neural pathway called the arcuate fasciculus.

(4) Koelsch, S., Gunter, T., Cramon, D., Zysset, S., Lohmann, G. & Friederici, A. (2002). "Bach Speaks: A Cortical Language-Network Serves the Processing of Music". *NeuroImage* 17: 956–966. doi:10.1006/ nimg.2002.1154. PMID 12377169.

(4) Brown, S., Martinez, M. & Parsons, L. (2006). "Music and language side by side in the brain: a PET study of the generation of melodies and sentences". *European Journal of Neuroscience* 23 (10):2791–2803. doi:10.1111/j.1460-9568.2006.04785.x. PMID 16817882.

(5) Daily News   http://www.dailynews.com/education/ci_ 16599265 Dana Bartholomew Higher Learning Report: LACCD lags in granting AA degrees and sending students to four-year schools 11/13/2010.

(6) LiveScience.com Stephanie Pappas, Senior Writer: "70% of Science Award Finalists Are Children of Immigrants" 05/29/2011.

(7) http://www.huffingtonpost.com/2010/12/07/us-falls-in-world-education-rankings_n_793185.html

The three-yearly OECD Programme for International Student Assessment (PISA) report, which compares the knowledge and skills of 15-year-olds in 70 countries around the world, ranked the United States 14th out of 34 OECD countries for reading skills, 17th for science and a below-average 25th for mathematics.

(8) cnsnews.com http://cnsnews.cloud.clearpathhosting.com/commentary/article/pat-buchanan-dumbing-down-america

CPSIA information can be obtained
at www.ICGtesting.com
Printed in the USA
LVIW011429030512
280241LV00001B